Lean In

LEVERAGE YOUR INFLUENCE FOR MINISTRY IMPACT

Lean In: Leverage Your Influence for Ministry Impact

published by Kidmin Academy

edited by Tina Houser

copyright ©2018

ISBN: 978-1-943294-84-8

cover design by Vanessa Mendozzi

CONTENTS

INTRODUCTION

Leaders Are Influencers

A LEADER IS SOMEONE who influences others. That sounds pretty simplistic, doesn't it? But, when it boils down to it, that's what leaders do. I've seen a 2-year-old leader running around the toddler room of our church. No one was running until that one particular "influencer" began to run, and then all the kids followed suit. I've seen a rowdy group of fourth grade kids calm when the oldest boy moved close to the teacher and demonstrated his quiet attentiveness. I've witnessed one elderly man at the church sport a positive attitude about the drastic change the pastor proposed, and the set-in-concrete naysayers suddenly supported the idea. What caused each one of these people to have such power? They were influencers, despite their age. They were leaders.

Everyone has been subject to sitting under both good leaders and bad leaders. It's wise for you to remember that those who have the quality of leadership ... will lead. They will find someone to lead. It's up to those who are raising up leaders to decide what kind of leader they will be. What kind of influence will you have over their future leadership? Hitler was a born leader who didn't have people surrounding him to mold his leadership skills in the right direction, whether that was on him as a child or as an adult. Leaders will lead. The desire to lead needs to be satisfied.

Talent. There are people who are born with leadership as part of who they are. It's a talent that's in their DNA. As I observed my grandtwins (a boy and a girl) in their playtime as toddlers, it was obvious which one led the other. If you wonder why the same people seem to end up as the chairperson, director, or head of programs, it's because leadership comes natural to who they are.

Spiritual Gift. There are people who God has given the spiritual gift of leadership to. Although they've never felt like a leader or been in a position of leadership, out of left field, God gives them the supernatural ability to motivate others and move them toward a common vision.

Learned. And there are people who are in a position where they are required to lead others, or they simply have that desire. They need to "learn" leadership from the very foundation. Back to the grandtwins ... the one who is not naturally a leader is learning leadership skills and has become quite an influencer among her peers.

Within the kidmin world, there are people who lead a group of five children and those who lead a team of 12 adults who minister to multitudes of kids. Despite how you came into your ability to lead (a talent, a spiritual gift, or learned), there's always room for you to improve your leadership skills. " ... *If one has the gift of being a leader, he should try hard when he leads ...*" (Romans 12:8, ICB).

Lean In has been compiled by a variety of kidmin warriors. They wrote with you in mind as a kidmin leader—volunteer, teacher, director, pastor. If you're sincere about living out Romans 12:8, then you'll want to do whatever needs to be done to develop each aspect of leadership. Some of the chapters in *Lean In* will address areas of leadership that you feel very comfortable with. Read them and give yourself a high-5. Others will expand on topics that are extremely challenging for you. Lean in and take notes. Take every opportunity to exercise that area of leadership. Make a plan that focuses on mastering that property.

When I think of "leaning in", I think of someone edging forward with their head slightly tilted to make sure they hear every word. God, in His extraordinary, unimaginably vast wisdom, has called you to lead His children to Him. Sit on the edge of your seat. Read each word. Underline and write in the margins. Make sure you take it all in. Lean in to what God is ready to teach you in order for you to become the leader He wants you to be.

Lead well,

Tina Houser

chapter 1

WATCH WHERE YOU'RE GOING

Developing and casting vision in ministry

BY MICHAEL BOWEN

RIFTING AIMLESSLY LEADS TO NOWHERE. Without a goal, without a purpose, without direction you're lost. Proverbs 29:18 encapsulates this in a broader, spiritual realm, *"Where there is no prophetic vision the people cast off restraint but blessed is he who keeps the law"* (ESV). Perhaps you know it better in the King James version, *"Where there is no vision, the people perish."* Without that direction provided by God and the prophets, the people cast off restraints and do as they desire; they do what is right in their own eyes. In ministry, there must be a clear understanding of the purpose of why you're doing what you're doing. This understanding brings direction, focus, and unity. Leaders in ministry must define their vision (why you do what you do) before they can define how to get there (what you are doing).

When my dad taught me to mow the lawn, I compared my crooked lanes in the grass to the straight lines of my father. I asked him how he kept his lanes looking so straight while mine were so crooked. He revealed that the secret is to pick a point in the distance and keep your focus on it, walking toward that specific point. If you only look at the spot directly in front of you, then your lines will be crooked. But if you determine the point in the distance to where you will walk, your lines will be much straighter.

In the same way, directors of children's ministry must pick a point on the horizon as your target to keep the ministry going straight toward that goal. You must have a vision for what it is you wish to accomplish in the ministry before you can figure out the best way to achieve that target. This aim usually mirrors and complements the vision of the church itself, but with its specific target audience (children) in mind. In other words, for children's ministry, the goals are similar to that of the church as a whole, but the process is made appropriate for accomplishing with the ages and abilities of children as their base consideration. While an adult ministry might go on an international mission trip, a children's ministry would talk about the mission, pray for it, and maybe collect some items for the mission team to use while traveling. The children are made aware of the international outreach, but they are personally involved in an age-appropriate manner. (There are now family mission trips that make an international experience appropriate for kids.)

Do you know the prayer statement of your church? Usually it's a one-line summation like, "Helping those who don't know Christ come to know Him; and those who do, become more like Him." This statement is missional (reaching the lost), and it is discipling (teaching and equipping believers to grow in their walk by becoming more like Him) in its summary. Do you have a prayer statement for your area of ministry? You might have one like the church's statement, but if it's too broad, consider narrowing it to make it more specific. Whether you use the church's or develop your own prayer statement, knowing what it is will give you a target to determine if the work you're doing is in line with your goal.

Jesus gave a mission to the disciples just before He ascended into heaven. Acts 1:8 records, *"But you will receive power when the Holy Spirit has come upon you, and you will be my witnesses in Jerusalem and in all Judea and Samaria, and to the end of the earth"* (ESV). Jesus gave them a purpose, or a mission, to accomplish in His absence. They were given the task of telling others about what they had seen Jesus do and accomplish while they were walking with Him. They were to testify that He had indeed risen from the grave and is alive! They were His witnesses. This broad task could be identified as their prayer statement. We'll see in a little bit how Jesus gave them more specific ways to accomplish this task, but it's important to note that this verse lays the foundation for the actions that are recorded in the book "The Acts of the Apostles." It is the "why" they are doing what they do in spreading the good news of Jesus' death, burial, and resurrection. To translate this into your ministry with children, you must first know what your prayer statement is.

As you determine your prayer statement, compare what it says with the dynamics of your current ministry: Does the work you are doing fall in line with the vision? If your prayer statement is missions oriented (to reach the lost), but your ministry doesn't do evangelistic outreach, does the statement need to be adjusted to fit your ministry (are you more discipleship-oriented?) or is there something about the ministry that needs to be adjusted to make it more evangelistic? When you have a clear picture of your ministry, develop a prayer statement and see if the actual work of the ministry is headed toward that goal. It is extremely important to evaluate the methods to ensure that they are in sync with reaching the target. The time that you have with the children entrusted to you is too brief to do "busy work" and miss the opportunity to share the Gospel or build relationships to encourage discipleship.

Ask yourself, "What is the most important thing to accomplish in my ministry?" Is it to simply keep the children from hurting themselves and pass them back to their parents the way they came in? Is it to teach them good, moral values while providing a safe, fun atmosphere in which they can learn these important life lessons? Is it to teach them the virtues of Christian living and the expectation to live a life holy to God? Or, like the Great Commission, is it to share the good news of salvation and teach how they can have a restored relationship with God?

How will you achieve the goal you have established? As you write out and evaluate your mission statement, consider what the method is that you'll use in order to accomplish the fine-tuned statement you have established? What benchmarks do you expect to see throughout the year to help you know you're on target? How will you communicate these goals and benchmarks to your leaders, your families, and to the children themselves?

How you accomplish the process of achieving your prayer statement is as important as establishing the statement in the first place. The method you use can determine the probability of success. Having established a prayer statement, design a framework of goals that you can use to measure your progress. These goals must be attainable, specific, and measurable. Where the vision was broad, the goals within the vision should be precise. Is your vision to reach the lost? Then how do you accomplish it? Do you have regular outreach events to build relationships with those outside of church fellowship? In what ways are you reaching into the neighborhood to invite families, who aren't already part of the church, to these outreach events? Who oversees follow-up? Are you using multiple forms of contact? How many attempts will be made to continue contact? The more specific the method (a particular event), the more precise should be your goals. By being mindful of the overall vision, your specific events will reflect the broader purpose of the ministry itself.

Let's return to what Jesus instructed His disciples. You already saw the broader mission that He gave in the book of Acts. Let's see what else Jesus told them. Mark 16:15 records Him saying, *"Go into all the world and proclaim the gospel to the whole creation"* (ESV). Matthew 28:19-20 teaches us He also said, *"Go therefore and make disciples of all nations, baptizing them in the name of the Father and of the Son and of the Holy Spirit, teaching them to observe all that I have commanded you"* (ESV). Both verses contain an evangelistic command. The followers were supposed to spread the Gospel and baptize those who believed. This is the primary duty of a believer. You're each called to tell others that Jesus' death, burial, and resurrection is the only acceptable payment for your sins and provision to a restored relationship with God. However, that wasn't their only task. Matthew's statement shows that they were to make these new believers disciples, and they were to teach these disciples to obey all that Jesus commanded them (including this final command)! Therefore, Jesus' instructions were evangelistic in that they were to share the good news, and they were discipleship-oriented in that they were to teach and equip these new believers. These two facets of ministry encompass the goal of the Church, and all local church prayer statements should incorporate them.

Most ministry goals align with evangelism or discipleship, which is a good thing. Given to the disciples with the intention to pass them on to the Church, these were never meant to be undertaken individually! Nor should you be attempting to accomplish these things alone. The Body of Christ is designed to be dependent upon others as you work in community to build and strengthen the Body through the work you do for Jesus Christ. Are you working in tandem with others? Not just doing the work together, but this evaluative process of seeing the vision and comparing it with the work being done. Are you aware that the work is to accomplish this goal, or are you doing the work simply because it needs to be done? Communicating the vision to others will give you co-workers who can help to regularly evaluate the direction the ministry is going, but it will also give motivation to them as you help them see the work that they are doing is not just filling a hole in a timeslot. Mission-minded volunteers are motivated to continue doing the work that has an eternal impact.

Having developed a mission statement, you need to learn it, live it, and teach it. Teaching others the importance of the work (why we are doing it) provides focus for them and unity in ministry. When composing the phrase, think how it sounds. Can alliteration or assonance help give a poetic tone to the statement? Perhaps, consider creating a call and response with the mission statement to help leaders and children commit it to memory. This has the added benefit of turning it into a chant or cheer, adding to the excitement of the truth. Since you are in children's ministry, let's incorporate multiple modalities of learning and assign motions as well.

Repeat your mission statement often. Teach the mission statement, it's origin and purpose, when on-boarding new volunteers and welcoming new families. Begin staff and volunteer meetings by reviewing it. Include it in formal communications such as emails or fliers. Hang it on the walls. Put it into practice and teach your leaders and families to view the ministry through the lens of the statement. When someone suggests an event, or if someone asks about a curriculum component, walk that person through the discerning process by asking them to compare the outcome of that addition or change to the mission statement.

Evaluate your ministry both mid-year and at the end of the season by asking your team and parents: Were benchmarks passed? Goals reached? The mission statement lived out? Ask them to contribute means to better align the children's ministry to the overall ministry of the church by further living out the mission statement in practice. Ask for testimonies throughout the year, both big and small, to highlight evidence of the vision taking root in mission practice. In this way, you create an intentionally disciple-making culture in your children's ministry. Keep your eyes focused on that fixed-point out over the horizon, casting a clear vision through continued communication and use of your mission statement.

Michael (and Michelle) **Bowen** direct Multiply Ministries as faith-supported missionaries with CMConnect, equipping the local church to develop disciple-makers through online training, conference speaking, and workshops. As a homeschooling family, they cherish the ability to travel in both North and South America while ministering to others. When not teaching about practical theology in children's and youth ministry, they love investing in their family by going camping, playing board games, and enjoying theater.

chapter 2

HIGH IMPACT

Leading up

BY AMY GOBLE

YOU ARE CALLED TO CHILDREN'S MINISTRY. That means, you're not aiming to be the senior pastor or the Big Kahuna. The idea of being able to say, "Go do this!" and it happen, may never happen! God has given you something even more powerful than a big title ... something that's even more impactful ... influence! And leading up is all about influence.

There's a way to lead and lead well from your current position. Remember Daniel? He wasn't in charge, yet God used him to change a nation. Remember Joseph? He was in jail (not in charge) when God used him to influence Pharaoh. Remember the disciples? They were average guys who God used to spread Christianity to the world! Yes, you can, as a kids' pastor, use your influence to lead up and see huge changes in your churches and communities.

There are 7 keys to leading up and having a high impact.

1. KNOW IT WILL TAKE TIME! Great leaders say, "You can get anything done that you want. It just might take a long time!" Boy, is that statement true! It takes consistent messaging to get your ideas across. I once worked for an executive pastor who was new to ministry. He loved Jesus but the idea of children's ministry was a fresh idea. In my enthusiasm, I assumed that it was possible to share all important information about children's ministry with him in a week or so. As you can imagine, it took longer than that! He wanted to focus on finances.

Once I realized it was going to take time, I asked for a monthly 20-minute meeting and showed up each month with what he loved the most—numbers and stories. I told the story of why our numbers were up, as a result of the first grader sitting in the back who came to church for the first time and got to hear how much God loved him! Or how a whole family started coming to church because their 3-year-old came home from preschool singing "Jesus Loves Me." This went on for months. Each time, I simply shared numbers and told the story behind those numbers. Eventually, he began to share those stories in staff meeting. He looked forward to hearing what was happening in children's ministry. It took a year! But, he became passionate about what God was doing in the kids' ministry, because he heard about it over and over and over for a year! It took time but it was worth it.

2. MAKE A PLAN! Every time you want to lead up, ask yourself, "What will leadership respond to?" and "What do they value?" A few years ago, a large church in our area was using handwritten sign-in for kids' ministry. "Why do you use a handwritten system?" I asked. They told me it was because the finance pastor didn't see a need for a computer system and didn't want to spend the money. They had tried for 4 years and were nowhere on getting him to understand. I asked if we could try asking again. Here was the opportunity to lead up.

All that was needed was a plan! For this leader, what he valued was charts, numbers, and good insurance. We immediately called one of the children's check-in companies and asked for all of their stats ... you know ... the ones with charts that show you why keeping kids safe is important. We ended up with pages of research, numbers, and charts that showed how "at risk" the kids were since the church was on a large freeway near a large airport. It would be very easy for someone to leave with a child and disappear. I brought that to the finance pastor and showed him all the charts. Within a week, the new computer system was in place! He needed someone to speak his language, to tell him why the church needed the system in a way that he could understand! That is leading up!

3. NEVER ASSUME! All professionals have their own vocabulary and children's pastors are no exception. Still to this day, if I forget, I will go into my pastor's office and start talking about ratios, volunteer polices, and video games! What I receive in return is a very blank stare and my pastor saying, "Slow down, Amy. What are you talking about?" One very effective way to lead up is to not assume your leader lives in the same children's ministry world as you. In fact, it might be safe to assume that they do not live in the same ministry world. So with each meeting and each point of contact, begin to train them on your world. Speak in terms that an "outsider" can understand. My friend calls it, "putting the cookies on the bottom shelf." They will learn. Using clear words and communication is a great foundation for leading up. For example, instead of saying, "We met all our ratios, Kidmin app worked, Fred didn't cry, and everyone showed up," you can say, "All the kids were in a safe environment, the check-in technology worked perfectly, saving parents time at check-in, a new guest to the nursery went in without any issues, and since all the volunteers were there, I was able to attend service." Saying it in a simple way will help your leader understand and follow what you're celebrating and trying to communicate!

4. GIVE UP THE CREDIT! After 14 years in kids' ministry, here is what I've learned, "You can get anything done, as long as you don't care who gets the credit!" Have you experienced that before? You share an idea with a co-worker and 3 months later they have a great idea—your idea! It can be very frustrating, but it can also be very effective. If you set your mind to simply getting ministry done without fighting for credit, you'll be astonished at all that will be accomplished! Your mind picks up ideas from multiple sources. You get inspired by the things people say or the things you see on Facebook or Pinterest! This happens with fellow staff members as well. They hear you say an idea and it goes into their brain for a few months where it rolls over and then blurts out as their idea in a staff meeting! You can use this to lead up!

Share your ideas whenever possible, knowing that they might return as belonging to another. Begin to help others "think." You can say things like "What would happen if we did this?" Or "Have you ever thought about doing this?" If you're leading them to think, they will most likely believe it to be their idea, but you can help shape their thinking! This can be very helpful in leading up. It can be shocking when the idea comes around again in a few months, but once a leader believes it to be their idea, they will support it to the end! Remember to be prepared in staff meeting to give up the credit, not fight for credit, and to support your leader on the idea. If you set your heart ahead of time, it can be extremely fun to support your (I mean your pastor's) idea!

5. BE CREATIVE! I had been a children's pastor for one year and was at my first church. I was so excited to minister to kids and to see God working in their lives. I loved my co-workers and was overwhelmed and thrilled at the same time! I had no idea what "leading up" meant or how important it would prove to be. I had an idea for changing our kids' ministry to family ministry. It meant a whole new way of doing ministry. I ran every single detail past my immediate boss. It never occurred to me to do more than that.

Then the day came when I was called into the senior pastor's office. He received the brochure I made announcing the new family ministry. This was the first he heard of it ... and he was not happy! I quickly realized that my boss had not shared any of what we were discussing with our pastor. I had assumed that information would be shared up and I quickly learned that unless I was leading up, no one else would take that responsibility for me. I could have been, and should have been, sharing this vision with my pastor the whole time. This was a big church. I really thought I couldn't get to the senior pastor, only to find out that's exactly what was needed.

I learned the crazy hard way, that sometimes you have to get creative in communication! The responsibility to communicate with leadership is yours! So ask yourself, how can I talk with that person? Be creative! It can be an email, or it might even be standing by their car! It can be taking them to dinner or it could be establishing a monthly meeting. It could be a notecard or talking to their spouse! It can be whatever it takes to lead up and get the information to them that they need to be able to lead effectively. Think outside of the box ... and start communicating!

6. PRAY! When I met him, I felt like he could never change. This was the boss we all talk about but hope we never have! He yelled a lot and I certainly preferred to not be in the office when he was around. I didn't realize I picked up the idea that God could not change his heart, until God reminded me to pray for him! So I started praying. I wasn't expecting much to happen but our God is amazing. There is nothing He cannot do! I prayed for months! Slowly but surely, my boss began to soften. God showed me what he was going through. Within six months, he was a new man. Yes, God had changed even him! And God had changed my heart in the process! There's no one outside the reach of God—even your boss! So start praying!

7. PARTNER WITH YOUR TEAM! You can't do it alone! Start spreading vision. That dream that God has given you, start sharing it with your ministry team. The more excited they get about it, the more it will naturally begin to spread up. It's called a "Grassroots Movement", and it's using the power of people to bring about change. Like we talked about earlier, it's not fast, but it's effective. If your ministry team becomes super excited about something, it can make even a senior pastor or leader take notice!

So, what do you do when you don't see results? Keep on going! Let's look at a few biblical examples. The Israelites were led out of slavery in Egypt after 400 years. Noah waited over 100 years for the flood to come while he built the ark. Mary and Martha watched Lazarus die before Jesus came and raised him to life! David was anointed king and then waited years to finally take that position. Israel waited thousands of years for the Messiah to arrive! God is not on our quick timetable. Wait, knowing that He has a big plan in place and is working, even when it feels like you can't see Him!

God is way more interested in the kids in your ministry than even you are! He loves them and gave His life for them. I've seen God do amazing miracles to help kids connect with Him! He is with you! He is for you! He will be right beside you. He will fight on your behalf. Walk in partnership with God and allow Him to guide you into effective and creative ways to lead up!

Amy Goble is the Children's Pastor at Bear Valley Community Church and the founder of KidsPray.tv. Her church staff says Amy is so perky that Disney comes to her to have a vacation! She loves all things glitter and sparkle, laughing, sleeping late on Saturdays, and good Mexican food!

chapter 3

MIGHT AS WELL FACE IT, I'M ADDICTED TO … LEARNING!

Being a perpetual learner

BY TAMMY JONES

"My mind is always racing, and always going and always working, and it's a gift and a curse." — Puff Daddy

THEY SAY THAT THE FIRST STEP in getting help is to admit that you have a problem. So here goes. "Hi! My name is Tammy and I am addicted to learning." If a class is offered in just about any subject, I will sign up to attend. I've taken classes on computers, painting, grant writing, wood etching, Photoshop. I have a cosmetology license and a Bachelor's degree in Elementary Education. Then there were the lessons in guitar and piano along with many workshops on various subjects such as graphic design and crafting machines, office administration, children's ministry, and Vacation Bible School. If I'm to be perfectly honest with you, then I will also have to confess to an unfinished Master's degree in Education that was left hanging out there somewhere.

That's me. Perpetual student. Lifelong learner. The word *perpetual* is defined as never ending; occurring repeatedly; so frequent as to seem endless and uninterrupted. Lifelong learning is the ongoing, voluntary, and self-motivated pursuit of knowledge for either personal or professional reasons. These are the words that should describe the way we all continue to learn. A very smart man by the name of Albert Einstein once said, "Intellectual growth should commence at birth and only cease at death." Safe to say that Albert was a supporter of lifelong learning! At the age of 87, Michelangelo is reported to have said, "Ancora imparo." The loosely translated meaning is, "I am still learning" or "Yet, I learn." Those of you who are perpetual, lifelong learners will gain knowledge, grow personally, and develop more self-esteem as you gain confidence in your knowledge. You will also find new opportunities, and experiences will open up because you have continued to learn.

Reading plays a big part in continued learning. Books, e-books, and audio books are convenient and affordable ways to continue learning on any schedule. Reading is also a far less expensive way to keep learning than taking classes or workshops. Remember the library? The library has books that can be checked out for free! Other great resources are e-books, magazines, blogs, podcasts, videos, and webinars. Here's a bit of great advice from a well-known doctor: "The more that you read, the more things you will know. The more that you learn, the more places you'll go." (Dr. Seuss) The National Reading Campaign once had a slogan that read, "You can borrow a book, but you get to keep the ideas."

Over the last few years I've read about ministries big and small and acquired many new ideas that can be re-imagined for the children's ministry at our church. "It is said that readers are leaders. Leaders are also learners. Every children's ministry leader I've had the privilege of meeting who is crushing it in their community or nation is committed to continual learning" (*How to Succeed as a Children's Ministry Leader,* Ricardo Miller). Reading leads to learning and learning leads to success.

As Christians each of us should continue to learn throughout our lives. *"Study to shew thyself approved unto God, a workman that needeth not to be ashamed, rightly dividing the word of truth"* (2 Timothy 2:15, KJV). Your knowledge and understanding of the Bible should be steadily increasing. Ministry leaders should always be seeking new ways to communicate the message of scripture to the children in their ministries. "Who dares to teach must never cease to learn" (John Cotton Dana). Dale Hudson of Relevant Children's Ministry writes, "The good children's ministry leader has completed a degree. The great children's ministry leader may have a degree, but realizes he/she will always be in school." If you want to be a great ministry leader, then you need to be committed to lifelong learning.

The benefits of being a lifelong learner for those in ministry are many. I will unpack just a few of them here.

Current. Being "current" doesn't mean wearing the latest fashions or having a really cool haircut, driving a sporty car, or using the latest buzzwords. Being current is knowing what's going on around you in your community and in the world. Are you aware of the things that the children in your ministry are facing at home or at school? What are the struggles and fears their parents are facing? What are the immediate needs of your community? What world events are impacting your students?

Staying current can help you know beyond your experience. Not a single parent? Talking to those who are may give you some helpful insights to share. Locate a workshop in your area to find some practical ideas on helping single parent families. Not a parent of a tween? Reading the latest information will help you understand tweens and their families. I'm not suggesting that you be a know-it-all. Sometimes, parents won't take advice seriously from a person who isn't a parent themselves. But if you have a knowledge base, you can speak to issues you don't have experience in yourself. If you do so respectfully and humbly you may gain an audience, especially if you already have a relationship.

Relevant. You will be someone who kids can relate to if you're constantly learning about their culture, current trends, and issues. The children's ministry leader who understands trends and culture will be more aware of the signs of an unhealthy situation. The kids in your ministry will be more open to you if they believe that you understand them and their world. (So stop that eyerolling and head shaking!) Being knowledgeable about their world shows them that you care and goes a long way in relationship building. If kids know that you care, they will extend you an invitation into their lives and be more likely to receive what you have to say. From that position, you can encourage them to grow, not just spiritually but in all other ways, while learning how to relate to others. That leads to happier and healthier lives. Children's ministry leaders need to "do everything we can to grow *ourselves* and create the right environment for others to grow" (Connected Principals blog, post by Jessica Johnson).

Knowledge. The constant pursuit of knowledge helps the children's ministry leader to know for the future. You have no way of knowing what you or your kids may be facing next year or even what may happen next week, but you can be prepared for situations ahead of time if you take the time now to learn about how to handle them. Ministry leaders should be prepared with checklists of procedures for handling emergency situations including all emergency numbers and routinely practice these procedures. You need to be prepared to handle serious situations that may not be considered emergencies but could be potentially dangerous or harmful. You become prepared for these kinds of situations by reading, listening, and learning how others have handled some of these same circumstances.

Continued learning helps you have information for parents. Leaders may be faced with situations that they themselves have never been through. Having some background knowledge of a variety of situations will at least be a starting place to enable you to offer encouragement and perhaps even make referrals to qualified professionals.

Understanding. A little knowledge of different backgrounds and customs will bring you some understanding of others and the continual broadening of that knowledge will bring you an even better understanding. The Cambridge English Dictionary defines "culture" as the way of life, especially the general customs and beliefs, of a particular group of people at a particular time. Music, arts, social habits, and cuisine are also parts of culture. In college, we were required to take a class on cultures from around the world. On a specified day each group gave a presentation on their chosen people group that included not only facts and photographs but also costumes, food, and music. What a wonderful day that was! Being a small town girl, I found the whole experience fascinating. In many cities around the U.S. various different cultures co-exist, but not in my town. We all knew each other and were all born and raised in the same area as our parents and grandparents, so there was really just one culture! In today's world with technology so prevalent and travel so readily available, the one culture situation is just not the norm any longer and hasn't been for some time.

Kid culture. Tween culture. Teen culture. Millennials. Generation Z. You need to be knowledgeable about more specific cultures than just knowing a few facts about people from other countries besides the one in which you live. You need to understand the different cultures in which the children you teach currently live. When you understand their culture, you become better able to understand them. You can better understand the way they dress, the way they speak, the way they behave, and the things they enjoy doing. This understanding helps you build better relationships with your ministry kids and with their parents. You may be able to help parents have some insight as well. But to be effective, you need to be constantly increasing your knowledge base.

Many ministry leaders are frustrated by declining attendance numbers and the seemingly lack of commitment by volunteers. However, just a small amount of research will bring understanding of new trends in church culture. Trends that, like social cultures, are constantly changing and do so quickly. The need for more and current information is essential if you are to effectively minister to your church family and to your community now and in the future. Understanding a current trend such as that of young adults who say they regularly attend church, who may in actuality only attend church once every four or five Sundays, will be beneficial. Leaders may still become frustrated over attendance numbers and volunteer commitments but understanding this current trend will enable leaders to examine their current situations and make decisions on how to best conduct ministry in the future.

People are people everywhere you go. When I learn of a situation or become involved in a circumstance, the first question I ask myself is, "Why did that person do that?" If I can come to some understanding as to what made the person say something or act in a certain way, then I can reconcile the situation within myself. This in no way will resolve the situation or make things better. But this personal resolution gives me a way to move on and enable me to extend grace to those people involved in the situation. Understanding people is important to be able to minister to them. Having some knowledge of human behavior allows you to deal more easily with difficult people.

New ideas. Perhaps you have just finished your degree and are feeling pretty confident in yourself. Maybe you feel sure that the knowledge you have obtained is all you will need to get out there and change the world for Jesus. But let me just tell you now that they don't teach you everything in college. Experience is an excellent teacher. However, a wise leader will always be a lifelong learner. Sooner rather than later, you need to become aware of what you do not know. When you depend on only current knowledge, you become stagnant and close yourself off to new growth and learning thereby missing out on new ideas and new experiences. Always be open to learning from the experiences and knowledge of others. There's something to be learned from almost everyone.

New perspective. Lifelong learners are open to new experiences. New experiences will bring new perspective. In 2004 I went on my first ever international mission trip. Here in the United States at that time, churches all around the country were building big buildings and exciting environments with treehouses and giant slides for the kids who came to their children's ministries. Those of us in smaller churches with smaller budgets were feeling a bit left out. Although our church had lots of things that many did not, we were still no match for those larger churches. After arriving in Lima, Peru we were a bit shocked at the lack of available tools for ministry. However, even after seeing their need, in the back of my mind I remained a little jealous and upset by our lack of resources. The next day our team went to a village where a lady from the local church we were partnering with lived. Elke and her family lived on the hillside in a small home that was pieced together from whatever materials they could find. Her home was crowded with children from the village sitting all around her small room. Elke was using some materials from church to teach the neighborhood children who could not afford the bus fare to come to the church. She was sitting at the table with one coloring sheet slowly tracing it onto a blank sheet of paper using her one and only sheet of carbon tracing paper. One sheet at a time. Some children were happily coloring while others waited patiently for their coloring sheet to be ready. All the while they were listening carefully while she taught. She taught them about Jesus using virtually nothing except love, and was doing a fabulous job of it too! I was broken and convicted. I had been so caught up with wanting the latest and greatest things and felt that if only we had them then we could do the greatest job ever ministering to the kids. I. Was. Completely. Wrong. Humbled and contrite, I immediately repented. This experience gave me a whole new perspective on how we should do ministry. Ministry should come from the heart, not from the pocketbook.

So be committed to the voluntary, self-motivated pursuit of knowledge. Let your learning be so frequent as to seem endless and uninterrupted. Let it be perpetual. If you plan on being the best children's ministry leader that you can be, continue learning. Learning is preparation. "Spectacular achievement is always preceded by unspectacular preparation." (Robert Schuller) Keep learning. Keep preparing. You will be spectacular!

"The beautiful thing about learning is nobody can take it away from you." – B.B. King

---

Tammy Jones is the children's minister at Cove Creek Church in Glencoe, AL. She will do anything to get the point across to children that Jesus loves you!

chapter 4

LEAD WITH A TOWEL

What does servant leadership mean?

BY ASHLEY KUHN

D O YOU WANT TO BE A GREAT LEADER? Of course, we all do! You want to serve Jesus with all you've got and be the best you can be for His glory alone. To be a great leader, you must lead with a towel in one hand. Leaders are not "lords" over their team; instead, they should be servants of the team. The Bible says you should, *"Serve one another humbly in love"* (Galatians 5:13b, NIV). Ministry is definitely not a one man show; you need each other. Leadership is not about being the best. Leadership is about making every person on your team better. When your team is succeeding, you're succeeding. The best way to lead your team is to lead with a towel.

WASH THEIR FEET.

Jesus Christ Himself embodied perfect servant leadership. You should strive to duplicate His example of putting others first at all times. Jesus lived with a towel in one hand. He demonstrated time and time again what it means to be a servant leader. While disciples argued over who would be the greatest in the kingdom of heaven ... Jesus taught them that the first shall be last. When James and John were scheming to make sure they would sit by Jesus in heaven, Jesus replied *"Not so with you. Instead, whoever wants to become great among you must be your servant, and whoever wants to be first must be slave of all. For even the Son of Man did not come to be served, but to serve, and to give his life as a ransom for many"* (Mark 10:43-45, NIV). He even got so desperate to get it into the disciples' thick heads that He got down on His hands and knees and washed their dirt-caked feet like a servant.

> *"Jesus knew that the Father had put all things under his power, and that he had come from God and was returning to God; so he got up from the meal, took off his outer clothing, and wrapped a towel around his waist. After that, he poured water into a basin and began to wash his disciples' feet, drying them with the towel that was wrapped around him. He came to Simon Peter, who said to him, 'Lord, are you going to wash my feet?' Jesus replied, 'You do not realize now what I am doing, but later you will understand'" (John 13:3-7, NIV).*

In taking off His outer garments, Jesus showed that His position of power within the group was not what was really important. Rabbis (or teachers) wore a special cloak with tassels on the corners. Their clothing indicated their status or leadership role. Jesus took off the outer robe and wrapped a servant's towel around His waist. By taking off his outer clothing and putting on the towel, Jesus was basically providing an object lesson for the disciples. It was as if He was saying, "Guys, really, status is not important. I'm the leader and I'm making Myself look like the servant. Do you see the symbolism here?" He wanted the disciples, and you, to understand that to be a leader you must first humble yourself and be a servant.

When Jesus took up the servant's towel and began washing the disciples' feet, He did it as a radical illustration to prove His point. Take a moment to think about it ... God himself, the Creator of the Universe, the King of Kings, the Lord of Lords, humbled Himself to the form of a human. And not just that! He then got down on His hands and knees to serve those whom He came to save. I'm telling y'all, "That'll preach!"

Jesus's use of the towel teaches us to serve God by serving others. When He was done washing their feet, He told them to wash each other's feet.

"When he had finished washing their feet, he put on his clothes and returned to his place. 'Do you understand what I have done for you?' he asked them. 'You call me 'Teacher' and 'Lord,' and rightly so, for that is what I am. Now that I, your Lord and Teacher, have washed your feet, you also should wash one another's feet. I have set you an example that you should do as I have done for you. Very truly I tell you, no servant is greater than his master, nor is a messenger greater than the one who sent him. Now that you know these things, you will be blessed if you do them'" (John 13:12-17, NIV).

Leading with a towel means serving others, not so they will serve you back, but so they will serve others. *"Submit to one another out of reverence for Christ"* (Ephesians 5:21, NIV). The metaphor of leading with a towel can go on and on.

GET YOUR RALLY TOWEL FLYING

Have you ever been to a sporting event where the fans have rally towels? They all, in unison, wave their rally towel, hoot and holler, encouraging their team. As a leader, you need to be your team's biggest supporter. You need to rally behind them. You need to encourage them! Empower your team to try new things. Let them take the lead. Encourage them to try new things. Share with your church all the times when your team "wins." Get the church excited for the kids' ministry team, too!

You know that the Bible tells you, *"Therefore encourage one another and build each other up, just as in fact you are doing"* (1 Thessalonians 5:11, NIV).

WIPE THE EGG FROM THEIR FACES.

This metaphor seriously makes me giggle every time. Back in the day, when actors performed a play, if the audience didn't like it, they threw eggs or tomatoes at the actor? Hopefully, no one in your church is throwing eggs at your kidmin team, but if they are, stand up for that person! You empowered them to do something to advance the kingdom of God. If it didn't work out, or it was an outright failure, encourage them to try again. Never speak badly about your team in public. Always praise them in public and lovingly critique them in private. If no one in your team is failing, maybe they're not taking big enough risks? Failure is an inevitable part of ministry. When you try something new and fail, you learn from your mistakes and get better next time. Work together to encourage one another even when you fail. *"If either of them falls down, one can help the other up. But pity anyone who falls and has no one to help them up"* (Ecclesiastes 4:10, NIV).

WIPE THE SWEAT FROM YOUR BROW.

There are times when being a good leader means getting down to the hard work and sweating in the trenches with your team. Is your team setting up for VBS? You should be there blowing up the inflatable palm tree. Are they low on volunteers in the nursery? Take a turn changing a stinky diaper. Be "in the trenches" with your volunteers doing the hard work of ministry as often as you can. I remember attending a church camp meeting as a young girl. The speaker on the stage was dynamic! I thought he was a superstar. After the service, we had a cake reception for him and his family. As we were finishing up and talking, I watched him get up and go table to table. I assumed he was signing autographs or kissing babies or whatever it is that famous preachers do. When he came to our table, I was taken aback! He was clearing the tables. He asked if we had "any trash." He asked, "Do you need another refreshment?" "Did you get enough to eat?" I remember being thoroughly shocked to see him serving when he was the guest of honor. It reminded me of the verse, *"Whatever you do, work at it with all your heart, as working for the Lord, not for human masters, since you know that you will receive an inheritance from the Lord as a reward. It is the Lord Christ you are serving"* (Colossians 3:23-24, NIV).

WIPE THE TEARS FROM THEIR EYES.

As their leader, you need to be involved in your teammates' lives. You should be doing life with them. That means you will be with them in the good times and the bad. You will be the person they come to when they lose their job, they have to put the family pet down, they're struggling with infertility, their aunt is sick in the hospital. You need to stand with them during times of crisis. It's not easy, but it is so worth it! *"Carry each other's burdens, and in this way you will fulfill the law of Christ"* (Galatians 6:2, NIV).

DON'T THROW IN THE TOWEL

Leaders do not quit! And they do not let their team quit either. *"There is a time for everything, and a season for every activity under the heavens"* (Ecclesiastes 3:1, NIV). There's a time for everything, just like wise King Solomon said. Make sure your leaders are not quitting before it's their time to leave. Help them avoid burnout during their season of ministry in the children's department. However, you should not make them feel like they are stuck in the same job forever! Give them defined roles and expectations so they know that their ministry assignment is not a life sentence. Let them know you are expecting them to serve for a "season." I read a quote recently that really struck a chord with me, "I threw in the towel. God threw it back and said 'Wipe your face. You're almost there'" (Unknown). *"And let us consider how we may spur one another on toward love and good deeds"* (Hebrews 10:24, NIV).

USE THE BATH TOWEL IN THE KITCHEN

In ministry, you can very easily become narrowly focused on your area of the church and ignore the rest. Silo ministry is not the best approach. And, you've all heard it said, over and over again, that you are "better together," which means, you should serve each other as well. You might think, "Whoa, hold up! I don't have time to help the choir director sort through music." Or "I'm not called to teen ministry. I'm definitely not helping at their all-nighter!" But did you know that when you help stack chairs in the main sanctuary, or you commit to praying for your lead pastor, or you do whatever it is that you consider outside your normal job title, that you're doing it for the Lord? You are all one church. You succeed together; you fail together. You need to have each other's backs, even if that might mean picking up the pizza for the youth pastor! *"For just as each of us has one body with many members, and these members do not all have the same function, so in Christ we, though many, form one body, and each member belongs to all the others"* (Romans 12:4-5, NIV).

LEAD WITH A TOWEL

According to the Servant Leadership Institute, the definition of servant leadership is to turn the leadership model, that society drives you toward, upside down. "Servant leadership is a set of behaviors and practices that turn the traditional 'power leadership' model upside down; instead of the people working to serve the leader, the leader actually exists to serve the people. As a result, the practice is centered on a desire to serve and emphasizes collaboration, trust, empathy, and the ethical use of power. Its primary goal is to enhance individual growth, teamwork and overall employee involvement, and satisfaction." Sounds like the way Jesus leads, doesn't it? This is the way you should lead as well!

To be a great leader you must first be a great servant. Lead your team with humility and grace. Serve them in radical ways like Jesus did, washing the disciples' feet. Encourage your team. Stand behind them when they're winning and when they're failing. Get busy doing the hard work of ministry along with your team. Stand with them when they're in a season of sorrow or grief. Be their shoulder to cry on. Encourage them to persevere. Don't let them give up. Serve in other ministries. Do all you can to help your team succeed by serving. Encourage your team to lead with a towel as well.

Ashley Kuhn is a proud member of the MOB—Moms Of Boys. She has 2 little boys, ages 6 and 4, and is married to her high school sweetheart. She's a children's pastor at Shepherd Church of the Nazarene in Columbus, OH.

chapter 5

LET IT GO!

Release control and grow

BY CORINNE NOBLE

IMAGINE WITH ME FOR A MOMENT, a 12-year-old girl who felt a calling on her life to become a children's pastor when she was only 10. She wasn't really sure what that looked like, but she was ready to get started, grow, and lead. She was willing to do anything to gain experience to prepare for God's calling. She got her first chance to do ministry: leading worship in kids' church. She couldn't sing, she was super awkward, but her heart for worship was all in. That girl was me! I'm so glad someone allowed me to get up on stage at 12 years old, even though I wasn't as good as those who were more experienced.

Let's just be real for a moment—would you have allowed someone as inexperienced as I was to serve in your ministry? Would you have told me to find somewhere else to serve or to wait until I'm older? Are you willing to relinquish control of parts of your ministry to allow a team of imperfect leaders to grow up around you? Or are you having a hard time letting go?

Why is it so hard for us to release control in our ministries?

There are three main reasons leaders struggle with letting go and releasing control.

Reason #1: You believe it's your job to do everything. You tell yourself that your lead pastor is paying you to do the job and they put you in this leadership position. Your team is full of unpaid volunteers, and you don't want to burn them out or give them too much responsibility. It's not your job to do everything in your ministry. Ecclesiastes 4:12 (NLT) says, *"A person standing alone can be attacked and defeated, but two can stand back-to-back and conquer. Three are even better, for a triple-braided cord is not easily broken."* If two or three people are better than one, I would guess that logic applies to even more people. The more, the better. Instead of seeing your ministry as a burden or a task, present it as an opportunity for others to grow and be part of a life-changing ministry. Who would say no to that? You need to first change your own perspective of why you do what you do, then you can present the vision to others.

Reason #2: You think it will be easier to just do it yourself. Sometimes, I really do believe this is partially true. If you delegate something important to someone else, they may do it poorly or not do it at all. When a service, event, or program goes poorly, or fails, the responsibility falls on the leader of the ministry, even if they weren't the one who made the mistake. It may be tempting to keep all the "important" ministry tasks to yourself, but by doing so, you will never see growth in your ministry. It takes a team to grow a successful ministry. God created people with different talents and abilities. Those talents and abilities shine the brightest when you use them collectively to build your ministry.

Romans 12:4-8 (NLT) talks about the importance of coming together as the body of Christ to serve others. It says,

"Just as our bodies have many parts and each part has a special function, so it is with Christ's body. We are many parts of one body, and we all belong to each other. In his grace, God has given us different gifts for doing certain things well. So if God has given you the ability to prophesy, speak out with as much faith as God has given you. If your gift is serving others, serve them well. If you are a teacher, teach well. If your gift is to encourage others, be encouraging. If it is giving, give generously. If God has given you leadership ability, take the responsibility seriously. And if you have a gift for showing kindness to others, do it gladly."

Just as your human bodies need every part to work together, each of you has a different and unique purpose in the body of Christ. Stop trying to do ministry with just one hand when you could have all of the other body parts help make that ministry even better.

Reason #3: You think you do it best. Let's be 100% honest for a moment. You know this thought has crossed your mind about something in your ministry. I will be the first to embarrassingly admit that this thought has crept into my mind more than a few times. Maybe you're an amazing speaker and you don't believe anyone can preach a message as well as you can. Or maybe you're a passionate worship leader and you've always been the one to lead the kids into worship. Maybe you love creating set designs that wow the kids and parents in your ministry and you don't believe anyone could understand your vision as well as you do. While these statements could be true, this is a pride issue. The book of Proverbs is full of verses about pride and the negative outcomes associated with it. Proverbs 16:18 (NLT) says, *"Pride goes before destruction, and haughtiness before a fall."*

Now, take a moment to think of something you do in your ministry that you do really well. Then, think back to one of the first times you ever did it. Were you just as good as you are now, or did someone allow you to fail, learn, and grow in that area for many years to make you what you are today? Most of you would probably agree with the latter. Keep that in mind the next time you want to hold tightly to something because you believe you're the best person for the job.

Why is it important for you to release control in your ministry?

God wants you to grow. God has entrusted your ministry to you, but He cares more about your personal relationship with Him than about how successful your ministry is. If you want to know how to grow your ministry and extend your leadership, the answer is found in John 15:4-5 (NLT). *"Remain in me, and I will remain in you. For a branch cannot produce fruit if it is severed from the vine, and you cannot be fruitful unless you remain in me. Yes, I am the vine; you are the branches. Those who remain in me, and I in them, will produce much fruit. For apart from me you can do nothing."* If you're trying to lead your ministry out of your own strengths and abilities, the Bible is clear about why you are failing. You can do nothing without Christ.

It starts with you as the leader of your ministry. A ministry can only be as strong and healthy as its leadership. Are you taking time to grow your personal relationship with God outside of your ministry preparation time? God wants to grow and stretch you. It may be a painful and uncomfortable process, but growing pains often are. Ask God what He wants you to release control of. Make room on your plate by releasing some of those things to others so God can fill your plate with something new.

God wants to grow your team. You could be the most amazing kids' pastor/director in the world, but you can only be so effective doing ministry on your own. God has called each of you to equip others around you to do ministry. Did you realize that one of your main jobs as a pastor or teacher in the church is to equip others to do the ministry? You were never meant to do the ministry by yourself. Ephesians 4:11-12 (NLT) is clear about this, *"Now these are the gifts Christ gave to the church: the apostles, the prophets, the evangelists, and the **pastors** and **teachers**. Their responsibility is to equip God's people to do His work and build up the church, the body of Christ."* I don't know a single kids' pastor who would say they already have enough volunteers. You all want more volunteers to add to your teams. Is it possible that one of the reasons you don't have enough volunteers is because you're unwilling to release control and step out of the way for them to lead?

In my ministry, I know my team will rely on me and allow me to hold onto the control of the service if I want to. I know it will hurt their confidence in their ability to successfully lead if I step in and "fix" things or take over when they're struggling. It's my responsibility as their leader to train them, allow them to fail, and help them to grow. Delegate true responsibility instead of "tasks" or "jobs" to volunteers who have been on your team for a while and have proven to be faithful and trust-worthy. Responsibility for a larger piece of the ministry will create personal ownership. You don't want your team to feel like they're doing tasks for your ministry. Instead, help them own a part of the ministry. You need to change the way you talk about your ministry. It's not "my ministry"; it's "our ministry."

God wants to grow your ministry. I'm not just talking about numerical growth, although that is something He can do if you're ready for it. God has called you to help the kids in your ministry grow spiritually. Teaching is great, but you have to disciple your kids to see true growth. Discipleship doesn't happen in a large group setting! Every kid in your ministry needs to know that one person really cares about them—someone who knows their name, what their interests are, what their home life looks like, and takes the time to pray with them and for them. Can you do that for every kid in your ministry? If you have fewer than ten kids in your ministry, the answer might be yes, for now, but I know you don't want to stay there numerically. You want your ministry to grow. If you want to see the kids in your ministry grow to love God more and more, you need to release control and allow someone else to be that one person who really knows them. Jesus taught the crowds, but He only discipled twelve. Crowds of people wanted to follow Jesus, but He knew He could only focus His daily attention on a small group of disciples. He had been watching the crowds of people and saw a few He wanted to come and follow Him.

Mark 3:13-15 (NLT) says, *"Afterward Jesus went up on a mountain and called out the ones he wanted to go with him. And they came to him. Then he appointed twelve of them and called them his apostles. They were to accompany him, and he would send them out to preach, giving them authority to cast out demons."* Jesus chose to spend the majority of His time with twelve disciples and there were only three in His inner circle (Peter, James, and John). The number twelve is known in the Bible to signify completeness and divine arrangement. I believe you should follow Jesus' example, because it's the best one we've got. Who will you choose to be in your inner circle? Choose to pour into and grow twelve people at a time and pass this example onto your team.

Are you willing to let it go and release control of anything God asks you to? If the answer is "yes," get ready for God to grow you, your team, and your ministry. It won't be easy at first and the process could be painful, but that's okay. I would rather trust God and see what He can do with my life and ministry than keep control and lead out of my own strength.

Corinne Noble is a curriculum creator and a children's pastor in Arizona. She loves sharing her favorite kidmin ideas, set designs, and curriculum on kidmincorinne.com.

chapter 6

FEAR IS A FOUR-LETTER WORD

The faith challenge of personal change

BY LISSA PAULIN

THE ONLY THING CONSTANT IS CHANGE." (Heraclitus) The experience is common and expected, yet it often produces fear. You fear the unknown outcomes of the future. An unexpected change can lead to uncertainty. Still, you know that change moves you forward. As a believer, you have a longing for the metamorphosis of becoming a new creation. I love how the New Living Translation presents this verse in Romans: *"Let God transform you into a new person by changing the way you think."* The outcome of this change is that you *"will learn to know God's will for you, which is good and pleasing and perfect"* (Romans 12:2, NLT).

In the face of change, replace the thoughts of fear with specific truths and actions. Focus on the fulfilled promises of God, set firm priorities, follow a clear vision, embrace flexibility, commit to fervent service, and be in the habit of faithful prayer.

When change stirs anxiety, remember the promises of God fulfilled in His Word and in your life experiences. "I know whom I have believed and am persuaded that He is able." (Daniel W. Whittle) The refrain of this hymn expresses a simple and profound truth about the God you are pleased to know and serve. He is able. Throughout Scripture you see God making and keeping promises to those who seek Him.

- A promise of victory over sin from Genesis 3:15, Psalm 32:1, 1 Corinthians 15:57, and Revelation 19:1-16

- A promised home; a place of belonging in this life and for eternity presented in Genesis 35:12, Psalm 16:5-6, and John 14:2-3

- Unending love, mercy, grace, and faithfulness written in Lamentations 3:22-24 and 1 Corinthians 12:9

It's a comfort to remember that "My God is so great, so strong, and so mighty. There's nothing my God cannot do." In your daily time with God, you can ask Him to speak these promises over you. You can write them on notes tucked into your planner or stuck to the computer screen and bathroom mirror. You can *take every thought captive to obey Christ"* (2 Corinthians 10:5, ESV) without fear.

I have a sister in the Lord who has posted a simple piece of paper in her kitchen on which she builds a visual altar of praise to the Lord. Each time she recognizes something God has done to bring her good or to glorify Himself through her circumstances, she draws a stone. A few words describe the significance of each stone, and she watches her blessings stack up each day. Like Samuel you can lift up your own stones called Ebenezer and say, *"The Lord has helped us to this point"* (1 Samuel 7:12, HCSB). The implication is that based on this knowledge of the Lord your Helper, you can expect Him to faithfully see you through whatever comes next. You can replace the fear of change with faith. The Bible gives you a written record of God's promises fulfilled throughout history, and you can expect to see the same God at work changing your life and impacting the lives around you.

Change can feel threatening to your routine, but it doesn't have to be a destructive force in your life. Having firm priorities can anchor your thoughts and actions when circumstances are in flux. God reveals His plan for your time and energy in the greatest commandments: *"You shall love the Lord your God with all your heart and with all your soul and with all your mind. This is the great and first commandment. And the second is like it: you shall love your neighbor as yourself"* (Matthew 22:37-39, ESV). He personalizes this command as He has given each person individual skills, talents, passions, gifts, families, ministries, and interests. I categorize and order the important things in my personal life something like this:

1. God

2. Household/Family – spouse, children, extended

3. Church – relationships, commitments

4. Work

5. Neighbors/Outreach.

As you experience change, monitor the impact on these priorities. Your relationship with God should continue to grow as you have need of Him. Marriage and family were set up as priority social organizations from the foundations of Genesis. As a ministry leader, don't forget to protect your family time and plan your schedule accordingly. You can pray for your church. You should fulfill your responsibilities to the local body with commitment and contentment. *"Do all things without grumbling or disputing, that you may be blameless and innocent, children of God without blemish in the midst of a crooked and twisted generation, among whom you shine as lights in the world, holding fast to the word of life, so that in the day of Christ I may be proud that I did not run in vain or labor in vain"* (Philippians 2:14-16, ESV).

Prioritizing your time and energy is crucial for those who are volunteer leaders, bi-vocational kidmin servants, or full-time staff ministers. If you have an additional occupation, balancing the responsibilities of work and ministry can be the most challenging. Work may have deadlines, hourly requirements, and assigned tasks that are outside of your control.

It's helped me to center my thoughts on this truth: *"Whatever you do, do it all to the glory of God "*(1 Corinthians 10:31, ESV). I'm reminded to serve God as my master and to bring Him glory in the way I perform my work among believers and non-believers. In the office, the home, or the church, your attitude and actions should serve to honor the Lord rather than your own achievement. Many of you serve in full-time ministry. You need to evaluate the use of your time or resources outside of your on-the-clock hours. You need to be present for your family. You need to be still and quiet before the Lord. Pursue a deepening relationship with the Lord and seek His guidance for your own list of priorities for your personal life and ministry.

Change in your specific ministry and church can feel like chaos for leaders, volunteers, kids, or families. You also need to prioritize the tasks, events, and goals of your specific programs. Your work should build on a foundation statement of vision or mission for ministry. Work with pastors and key leaders. This is beyond how often to have kids worship or whether to have a verse memorization contest. Think bigger than your teaching schedule or curriculum for the year. What are the big picture goals of your church? What does that look like for the younger members of your church family?

For example, my local church mission is: win, build, send. I took that and wrote a simple vision for our Sunday school program. I want our aim to be winning kids to Christ, building them up in their faith and worldview, and sending them into their world—family, friends, school, and future—with a kingdom impact. I briefly outlined some of the ways these goals will be accomplished: frequent presentations of the Gospel; teaching on the character of God; building relationships between kids and God, kids and peers, kids and leaders; participating in missions; inviting friends to church. I want the kids in my ministry to feel safe physically and spiritually, and to know they are loved by God and by this church! Volunteers will feel empowered to meet these essential elements beyond successfully completing the planned lesson. You can feel confident in your objectives amid seasons of change in attendance, church staffing, volunteers, curriculum, or physical spaces.

"In his grace, God has given us different gifts for doing certain things well" (Romans 12:6, NLT). Many of you are gifted in leadership, administration, teaching, or service. Fulfilling your responsibility does not always mean controlling the people and processes around you. One thing I wish I would have learned years ago is to cultivate an attitude of flexibility. You must be realistic in the expectations you hold for yourself and others; reevaluate as necessary. The time required by various life responsibilities will keep changing.

I began in kidmin when I was young and single. I had plenty of time and enthusiasm. Moving into adulthood, starting a career, getting married, and buying a house expanded my to-do list while consequently limiting my unoccupied time. I'm now in the season of mothering three young children. I'm also a bi-vocational kidmin leader. I teach middle school half days, care for the needs of my family in the home, and serve many hours each month coordinating children's ministry at my church. I've had to learn to use my time differently to meet my personal spiritual needs, to feed my soul, and to feed the children in my care. I can find joy in caring for the needs of my family knowing that I am uniquely gifted to influence the children in my home.

I often think of all the things I wish I could do in my ministry. This has challenged me to involve more people to accomplish things I cannot do on my own, to plan more purposefully for now and the future of my ministry, and to recognize the faithfulness of God in my limitations. Ministry looks very different as a single 20-something than it does after a marriage, a move, the birth of a child, becoming a blended family, turning 40, an empty nest, a health need, a loss. Sometimes, you must redefine your view of success in ministry. As your life and ministry changes, flexibility will allow you to continue using your gifts well, seeking wisdom, and glorifying the One who *"gives generously to all"* (James 1:5, ESV).

You have heard the voice of the Lord tell us to *"let the little children come"* (Matthew 19:14, ESV). Be unmoved in your commitment to bringing young hearts near to God with all your strength, for all your life, through any change. God has already used changes to bring you to your current place of ministry.

The volunteer who coordinated the Sunday school program at our church wanted to hand off the leadership responsibilities to someone else. I was a faithful class leader, I had been helping prepare some of the curriculum already, and I had years of training in the field of professional education as well as Christian children's ministry. I was the obvious choice to take on the role, but I declined. No change needed in my life, thank you. I probably don't have the time. Three months later, I was vol-un-told that no one else could do it. They needed me. I agreed to take on the coordinator position, and things ran smoothly for quite a while.

A few years later, our small congregation stepped out in faith to plant a church. It was exciting, but it also meant sending approximately 20 adults to begin the work. My volunteer roster was significantly impacted. Other changes in our church leadership, attendance, and my family (babies!) over the years left me speeding toward burnout. I recall the year 2015 being particularly rough. I was overwhelmed, exhausted, and discouraged. I asked God to tell me who He wanted to really do this role well.

I heard about a small kidmin conference happening that fall. It was within my budget and my driving distance, so I registered. My husband wisely advised me that if I attended this conference, I should commit to leading the ministry for the remainder of the school year. Okay, fine. One more year. During one of the presentations at that conference, a slide appeared comparing volunteer thinking (my pastor called me and I can quit any time) with minister thinking (God called me and I can't quit unless God lets me). So I asked God to let me quit that year. He said, "No. I called you. I'm using you. I'm changing you. I'm at work." I committed that week to stay in kidmin unless God clearly called me away. I set my commitment on two specific verses that I hope will also encourage you to commit your life to serving God's kids. *"Never be lazy but work hard and serve the Lord enthusiastically"* (Romans 12:11, NLT). *"I will most gladly spend and be spent for your souls"* (2 Corinthians 12:15, ESV).

Above all, you are more than conquerors over fear when you draw near to the Lord who gives the victory. Expressing your anxieties, questions, hopes, and joys to God is your privilege as His dear sons and daughters. In seasons of change, you have this command in scripture: *"Rejoice in our confident hope. Be patient in trouble, and keep on praying"* (Romans 12:12, NLT). Be in the habit of kneeling before the One who is faithful.

"Call to me and I will answer you, and I will tell you great and mighty things, which you do not know" (Jeremiah 33:3, NASB). Replace the fear of change in your ministry with eagerness and longing to be amazed at what God will do. Plan your time and goals. Pursue your passion considering your priorities. Allow God to use a variety of circumstances, talents, and individuals to reach His people. Never give up. Persist in prayer. You can choose to see change as an opportunity for God to work in ways *"far more abundantly than all we ask or think"* (Ephesians 3:20, ESV). In His ministry, Paul repeated the words spoken to Habakkuk: *"Look and be amazed! For I am doing something*

in your own day, something you wouldn't believe even if someone told you about it" (Habakkuk 1:5, NLT). Are you ready to be amazed by the change God has planned for your heart, your kids, your mission?

Lissa Paulin really "fits" right in with kids since she's 5' 2", but that's a stretch! One of her greatest joys is having people to her home for a meal, so feel free to invite yourself over if you're ever in Wisconsin.

chapter 7

A PIRATE'S LIFE FOR ME

Setting objectives for your kidmin

BY BRITTANY NELSON

PIRATES ARE OUT FOR ONE THING: buried treasure. They plot, chase, and cheat their way to their desires until they are swimming in gold coins. And while I don't recommend doing any of that in children's ministry, pirates can teach you a little something about setting and pursuing your goals.

Pirates recognize that you cannot merely point the ship in the right direction. You have to do the jobs that make the ship move forward or it will be tossed around by the waves and end up far off course.

The children and families you serve are more important than buried treasure, and you have to take the time to intentionally think about the direction of the ministry that serves them. So, you set goals and make plans, but you often miss a key development: turning your goals into objectives.

What's the difference? Goals are general, broad, long-term dreams, like "I want the children in my ministry to be comfortable with prayer and enjoy praying to God." Objectives are more specific actions designed to accomplish a particular task within a set timeframe, like "I want to give each child the chance to pray out loud at least once over the next month." How do the two relate? Objectives are clearly defined, measurable steps to help you achieve a larger goal.

Imagine that your children's ministry is a pirate ship and you're the pirate captain (arr, matey!) Setting goals for your ministry helps steer your ship in the direction you want it to go and gives you a map of where you're headed. But objectives are the specific tasks and actions that propel the ship forward in the intended direction. Most people set goals but stop there, never articulating the objectives that will bring the overall goal to fruition. This leaves your pirate ship pointed in the right direction but just sitting, floating in the waves.

The best advice I've ever heard on goals came from a random leader at a Catalyst Conference. He said, "Think big, start small, keep moving." This mentality helps goals move into objectives so you can find the buried treasure of leading families and kids well.

Thinking big helps you identify the goals, starting small helps you set the objectives for those goals, and keeping things moving helps you persevere to the "X" that marks the spot.

Think Big. Goals are broad and general like a guide map, so as you set goals for yourself and your ministry, think big. This may be a task you complete on your own, or it may be one you complete with your ministry staff. As you're sailing the seven seas of children's ministry, the whole ocean is available to you, so don't hold back.

Start with prayer. (This really should be a given in our line of work.) Some of my favorite verses I pray when planning are Psalm 20:4, Psalm 33:11, Philippians 3:14, Proverbs 16:3,

Proverbs 21:5, and Matthew 21:22. I like to read through and pray these verses before every big planning session, just to focus my heart and invite God into the planning. Praying also allows the time for God to speak to me about His goals for the ministry, so I'm not limited by what my brain can come up with.

You can also think big by keeping the vision and mission of your ministry in mind. The short, memorable vision statement for my ministry was "Grow and Go." We wanted kids to grow in their relationship with Christ and go out and serve others in His name. Everything we did had to fit under that blanket statement and serve to help us accomplish that mission.

I started thinking of my ministry vision statement like a colander or pasta strainer, and I ran all new ideas, events, and activities through that filter. One hundred percent of the ideas and suggestions I heard may have been good ideas, but if they didn't fit within the overall vision of our ministry, then I couldn't afford to put my time, energy, and effort into them. So let your mission statement be a filter. Pour all your ideas through it, and see what sticks. All of your goals, no matter how small, should fit within the big-picture purpose of your ministry.

Part of thinking big is looking back. You have to evaluate the past to plan for the future. What went well last year? What was lacking? Where is an area you want to see growth in the ministry and in the children? What questions did you answer that may reveal a topic you need to address this year? To know where you're going, you have to know where you've been. Talk with your team, parents, and senior pastor about these questions, and evaluate a starting point.

If nothing was holding you back (not even a lack of budget or volunteers), what would you want to see happen in your ministry this year? You serve a God who specializes in doing the impossible, so dream big!

Start small. Now that you've got your grand plans and your guide map, it's time for the smaller details. Here is where you start transforming your goals into objectives with specifics, timeframes, and action steps. Weigh anchor! Hoist the sail! Come about!

One of the easiest ways to achieve your goals and make them actionable is to write them down. Studies have shown that when you write down your goals on a regular basis, you are 42% more likely to achieve them because it engages both the creative and logical parts of your brain. So write down your goals on sticky notes, in a journal, or in an email.

As you write your goals, there are a few key elements to include that can help them become objectives. Objectives are time-sensitive, so give each one a deadline. This helps with accountability and follow-through. Objectives are also measurable. You will know that you have achieved your objective because there will be evidence, so make sure to think through how you will measure and record success.

Use positive language. When you phrase your objectives negatively, you subconsciously imply that you're doing something wrong. So instead of saying, "Stop procrastinating," change the wording to "Stay ahead of my schedule." Putting a positive spin on the language of your objectives helps you feel excited about tackling them.

Look for the specific, next steps that will help you accomplish each objective. You can't jump from point A to point D without going through steps B and C first. And if you were really dreaming big, you may have to go through the entire alphabet from point A to point Z. Maybe a family VBS is one of your objectives. That's great! But if the families in your ministry aren't ready for that kind of change, it's going to backfire. Trust me.

During my first year of ministry, I came home from a children's ministry conference fired up about family ministry and ready to implement it at my church. I started planning a family VBS where parents would attend with their children for the week. I talked with my key parents, who seemed on board, worked to solve problems that would prevent families from coming, and launched the registration at our normal time.

Weeks went by, and with just 2 weeks left before the event, only 3 children had signed up. When we were used to having 75 kids at VBS, this number was low! I was deeply disappointed. Hadn't God given me the vision for incorporating parents into such a monumental event?

Why had it failed? Because I tried to force the families from one end of the family ministry spectrum to the other without easing them into the transition through smaller events and practices. I needed to start small. So I offered more single-day family events to try and let my families build up to the idea of a family VBS. This shift to family ministry is still a work in progress.

Some goals require a change in the church culture, and those kinds of changes don't happen overnight. Start small with the specifics of your goals to turn them into attainable objectives and take action steps toward the buried treasure.

Keep Moving. A pirate ship in the middle of the ocean does not have the choice to just give up and stop what it's doing when the seas get rough; it must continue on one way or another until it finds land. No matter what happens, keep moving forward. There will be storms, droughts, and winds along the way, but don't let them bring you to a halt. Continue pressing on toward your goals by completing your objectives, even if you have to take a different route than you were expecting. You may have to re-evaluate how you're going to get there, but keep moving.

Stay accountable by sharing your objectives with others and adopt an all-hands-on-deck approach. Now that you've written them down, talk them up! Who can you invite on the adventure with you? Will it be a co-worker, your senior pastor, a friend, or even a fellow kidmin leader through Facebook? How and when will you share these goals and objectives with them? Text? Email? Singing telegram? As always, be specific.

Then communicate your objectives for the ministry with your team, your volunteers, and the families you serve. This will invite them to be part of reaching those objectives and give them ownership within the ministry.

Also keep your objectives visible. I'm a big fan of sticky notes. Some of the notes from when I first started in children's ministry are still above my desk and that was 5 years ago! So whether it's a physical place in your office or a digital space on your computer, put your objectives in a place where you'll see them often.

The best motivation is positive motivation, so celebrate success. As you reach milestones along the way to your goals or even complete each objective, make sure to take the time to celebrate! Do your happy dance, share the good news, and celebrate the wins. This will give you the motivation to keep moving when things get tough and allow you to invite people into the great things God's doing in your ministry. Even if the accomplishment seems small, take the time to celebrate it.

Your Turn. Now that you've read about dreaming up goals and setting objectives to make those dreams a reality, it's your turn. Put on your eye patch (I know you have one somewhere), grab a pen, and use the spaces below to practice steering and sailing your ship toward the buried treasure.

THINK BIG

1) Start with prayer. Take time to invite God into your time of planning and ask Him to guide you, give you a vision for the future, and spark creativity.

_____

_____

_____

_____

_____

2) Write down your ministry's mission, vision statement, or purpose. Keep this in mind as your pasta strainer to set goals and objectives.

_____

_____

_____

_____

3) Evaluate last year. What went well? What needs to change? Did everything fit into and support the overall vision statement of the ministry? Is there something you should cut?

_____

_____

_____

_____

START SMALL

4) Based on your evaluations from last year, write down a broad, general goal for next year. Then fill in some specific details about the goal to make it an objective.

_____

_____

_____

Goal:

_____

3 smaller steps to start:

1. _____

2. _____

3. _____

How does this goal fit in my overall ministry vision?

_____

_____

_____

_____

How will I measure this goal?

_____

_____

_____

_____

Who will I share this goal with?

_____

Projected completion date: _____

5) Keep your goals and objectives visible. Where can you keep these goals so you see them every day? Copy the goal and its objective details from the previous step onto a sticky note, a journal, or even a Chick-fil-a napkin. Where can you keep this so you will see your goal often?

_____

_____

_____

6) End with prayer. Ask God to give you perseverance, endurance, and strength to help you accomplish the goals and objectives you've laid out. Ask for the people and volunteers to support you in ministry. Tell God how excited you are for what He will do in the year ahead.

_____

_____

_____

KEEP MOVING

This chapter has no ending because the ending is you, captain! Every couple of months, check back in with your objectives. Redirect where you have gotten off course. Celebrate what you have accomplished. And know that I am praying Psalm 20:4 over you as you think big to set goals, start small to determine objectives, and keep moving forward in the adventure that is children's ministry. Land, ho!

Brittany Nelson is the creator of DeeperKidmin.com, an online resource that equips ministry leaders to grow kids deeper in their relationships with Christ through engaging and affordable ideas. Her other adventures include trying to finish seminary, reading as many books as she can, volunteering with her husband's youth group, and drinking lots of tea.

chapter 8

THE WILLY WONKA GOLDEN TICKET

You are a phenomenal communications guru!

BY SHERRY CHESTER & DR. JOEL TIEMEYER

MOST, IF NOT ALL OF US, want a golden ticket. You long for the chance to have life revolutionized by something wonderful, like owning Willy Wonka's Chocolate Factory. Children's ministry leaders dream of having more than enough kind-hearted "Oompa Loompa" workers ready to help, an entire factory of creative sets as far as the eyes can see, and of course unlimited access to every type of awesome snack one could possibly imagine.

There is something far better than a **Willy Wonka Win** and certainly better than **World Wide Wrestling**, even though this feels like children's ministry many times. Also, it's far more helpful than the **World Wide Web**. There is a **WWW** that empowers you, yes you, to be a phenomenal communications guru. Effective and sustained communication is the golden ticket *"to equip the saints for the work of the ministry, for building up the body of Christ"* (Ephesians 4:12, ESV).

Now is the time to think and lead differently! Whether you have been in leadership for three months, three years, or three decades, let's visualize who you are and what is at the core of all you do. Everything discussed will evolve around five declarations about your wonderfully anointed life.

You are vision-full.

You are purposeful.

You are intentional.

You are relational.

You are tactical.

With this in mind, we'll share concepts that have revolutionized how you minister, work, and do life together as a church staff and family. You are a work in progress, yet willing to share how to build capacity and function at higher levels than ever before. Dr. Joel Tiemeyer, lead and founding pastor of The Way Bible Church (TWBC), introduced staff to this framework of leadership communication. Let's unpack this as it relates to ministering to children, families, and NextGen from infancy through 28 years old.

WWW Unfolds. Imagine for a moment a large blank square on a piece of paper. Better yet, draw one. Got it? Now place a big plus sign inside the box that divides the square into four equally distinct sections. Good job! In the top left box write the word "Impact." Next, in the top right corner write the word "Work." You're halfway there ... keep going ... you got this. Now, in the bottom left corner write the word "Effort." Lastly, in the bottom right corner write the word "Measure."

Impact (top left corner). Impact is what you want children and families to gain from a service or event. What does everyone need to leave knowing or experiencing? Does the service, event, or training contribute to a bigger picture of the mission statement and vision? As a phenomenal communications guru, you articulate the anticipated impact to people in simple and direct terms. Impact answers the question: How will this advance the kingdom of God?

Work (top right corner). Work is what is done on the actual day of the service or event. This includes setting up, tearing down, preaching, praying, worshiping, and all other things associated with ministering to children, families, and volunteers in anointed excellence.

Effort (bottom left corner). Effort involves all the prep work leading up to what will get done. This includes study time, lesson prep, collecting resources, scheduling volunteers, checking on kids, and equipping parents.

Measure (bottom right corner). How is impact measured beyond how many kids are present? How will the impact of a service be measured? How will impact be measured over time? You measure what you treasure. Knowing to what extent the lives of children and families are being transformed is paramount. Matrix matters as a vital form of communication.

By now you're probably thinking, "What about the **WWW?** What is **WWW** going to do to bring functionality into my life?" The suspense is getting to me! Hold on a little longer to grab this next concept. *Impact drives work and effort, not the other way around.* Read that again. If this gets out of order and consideration is given to the amount of work and effort it takes to pull something off, complacency will set in with the thought that "it's too hard" will take root. When the focus is on impact—advancing the kingdom of God—vision is realized.

For example, Pastor Joel knew TWBC was to host a Super Sunday at the County's Civic Center so people who typically do not go to church had a neutral place to experience Jesus. This would also give the church family time all together, since we have outgrown the facility and have multiple services. The impact was to reach the community, since Barna's most recent data shows only "4 in 10 (38%) Americans are active church-goers" (Church Attendance Trend Around the Country, May 26, 2017). Reaching people was the determining factor. We had to change how we thought and not focus on how much work, time, and effort it would take to pull off a service of this magnitude, with a free scrumptious buffet luncheon, and awesome activities for kids afterwards.

Knowing that impact drives work and not the other way around, it's time. Drum roll please. The **WWW** that is a game changer is answering **W**ho does **W**hat by **W**hen?

This applies to all facets of life and ministry when you're at work, at home, at play, or planning a vacation. **W**ho does **W**hat by **W**hen is all-encompassing, a lifestyle choice that when implemented daily makes you a phenomenal communications guru (happy face emoji).

Let's look at how this rolls out in light of the five declarations about your wonderful life we spoke over you earlier: 1. You are vision-full. 2. You are purposeful. 3. You are intentional. 4. You are relational. 5. You are tactical.

1. You are vision-full. How do you know that about you? The Word says, *"Where there is no vision the people perish"* (Proverbs 29:18, KJV). Another version shares it this way. *"Where there is no vision [no revelation of God and His word], the people are unrestrained"* (Proverbs 29:18, AMP). Since you're reading this chapter, you understand the need to share the vision and purpose of God. After all, He calls you friend, therefore you know what He wants. *"No longer do I call you servants, for the servant does not know what his master is doing; but I have called you friends, for all that I have heard from the Father I have made known to you"* (John 15:15, ESV).

God only anoints who He appoints. You are appointed for this time and season. How exciting! Remember, what you have seen, heard, and played over and over in your head 50 times already is not something people may know or even be aware that you're thinking on, because it hasn't been verbalized.

Look to see what God is saying. *"And the Lord answered me, 'Write the vision, make it plane on tablets, so he may run who reads it'"* (Habakkuk 2:2, ESV). Add value to the vision by explaining it to others in a systematic way. The vision, with a plan, done in the presence of God, causes people to buy in and feel confident moving forward. Refuse to assume that people know what you are thinking! Answer the **W**ho does **W**hat by **W**hen (**WWW**) in casting vision.

2. You are purposeful. This next sentence forever changed my ability to be all God has called me to be. Pastor Joel said, "We win, or we learn. It is never a loss." As I began to realize things do not fall into either a win or lose category, full of nagging comparisons, I could see myself the way God sees me. *"For we are his workmanship, created in Christ Jesus for good works, which God prepared beforehand that we should walk in them"* (Ephesians 2:10, ESV).

One of the most memorable songs as a teenage helper in children's church decades ago was entitled, "I Am a Promise" (Bill and Gloria Gaither, 1975). It bears repeating, for you are full of potentiality.

I am a promise.
I am a possibility.
I am a promise with a capital "P".
I am a great big bundle of potentiality.
And I am learnin' to hear God's voice.
And I am tryin' to make the right choice.
I am a promise to be anything God wants me to be.
I can go anywhere that He wants me to go.
I can be anything He wants me to be.

I can climb the high mountains.
I can cross the wide sea.
I'm a great big promise you see!

It's not about making the "big ask" of others. Things like recruiting, scheduling, training, and a myriad of undertakings involving people isn't something to be dreaded or procrastinated. Why? People want to be "everything God has called them to be." Respond to them just like Jesus. Lovingly say, *"Come and follow me, and I will transform you into men [and women] who catch people for God"* (Matthew 4:19, TPT) [brackets added]. Communicating specifics of Who does What by When causes people to want to do the greater works of helping with children and families in various ways. Change your perspective.

The best thing to do with any task that has several different moving parts is to apply **WWW.** Who does What by When? This demystifies and breaks things down into doable bite-size pieces of chocolate. When you share, everyone is fulfilled. Now that's a golden ticket!

3. You are intentional. Consult with volunteers weekly who are invested in ministering to children. One way to strategically map out moments is to have a system in place for planning Who does What by When. For instance, each week's meeting has a specific focus.

Week 1: 30 days out

Week 2: 60-90 days out

Week 3: 3-6 months out

Week 4: 6 months to a year out

Week 5: Deliberately go play and do life together

Weekly meetings involve paid staff and volunteers who are in high functioning kidmin leadership roles. Restate the primary focus for each week. Celebrate what's taking place and look forward to what's happening next with a visual agenda. A visual handout of the agenda is fundamental to the success of the meeting. Also denote how much time will be given to each topic to help keep everyone focused. Diligence deserves a reward. That's where four months with five weeks comes into play.

Since our team meets on Tuesday mornings for 60 minutes, the next 5th Tuesday will be when we do Group Life (you plus two or more) together. The plan is to take the four people who are currently on the leadership team, along with three more we will be formally onboarding that day, to play Top Golf and eat lunch together in a city about an hour away.

You may be asking yourself, "How can they do this when there is so much to do?" Both time and resources have been intentionally allocated to build relationships and celebrate people. A team that prays, plans, and plays together stays together. *"A joyful heart is good medicine"* (Proverbs 17:32, ESV). Purposefully cultivating a rapport with staff and volunteers is the springboard for developing authentic pastoral relationships with children and families.

4. You are relational. Jesus was all about relationships. He spent time alone with God daily and He was with people often. Give thought to who you will interact with weekly. As a communications guru, reach out to people in two distinct ways: Contacts and Connects. Then, have someone in ministry hold you accountable to this high level of communication.

A Contact is where you check in with an individual for 10-15 minutes tops. Stop by their workplace, visit with them at a store or other public place for a few moments. The goal is to: (a) genuinely let them know you appreciate and celebrate their life; (b) ask how you can be praying for them; and (c) let them know you're looking forward to seeing them for the weekend experience of celebrating Jesus together. Schedule time to connect with several individuals each week as it values and validates people in really great ways!

A Connect is a longer more intentional visit of 30 minutes up to an hour where you meet with someone at a local coffee or sandwich shop. This conversation is about getting to know the individual better and investing in them. Start with a, b, and c conversation points mentioned earlier. Then listen. Put the cell phone down. Be attentive and engaged. This is not a multi-tasking moment. People are starved for genuine relationships. Heidi Baker, missionary and CEO of Iris Global says it this way, "Stop for the one." You cannot meet with everybody. You can start with somebody today.

From a scheduling perspective, it may work best to meet in the mornings before the work day begins. For me, it helps to set aside one afternoon or day a week for contacts, connects, and community type of off-site meetings. On the same day, a quick 2- or 3-sentence note is recorded in Planning Center (an internet-based application that keeps staff and volunteers connected) on how the get-togethers went. The notes become a running record as to spiritual formation. In turn, this helps pastors pour into individuals at a high level. Communication takes place in several different ways.

5. You are tactical. The definition of tactical as an adjective means "relating to or constituting actions carefully planned to gain a specific military end" (dictionary.com). You equip the saints to advance the kingdom of God. Therefore, a plan is necessary. It is to be coupled with being practical. Being practical means "of or concerned with the actual doing or use of something rather than with theory and ideas" (dictionary. com). Who does What by When puts the thoughts and plans of God that He has specifically downloaded to you into action. (Woohoo!) You were destined to have a golden ticket and be a fabulous communication guru!

This is it—WWW. Who does What by When portrays your awesome communication guru skills as you recall the five declarations spoken over your life. Know where you're going and how you want to get there. Write it down so people understand the process. Give everyone enough time to comprehend the desired outcome and provide input. Value people and help

THE WILLY WONKA GOLDEN TICKET

them experience personal fulfillment, then you will be communicating in a way that draws all people unto King Jesus.

Sherry Chester, Children's Pastor at TWBC, likes to travel, decorate, and hang out with her honey of a husband, their 6 successful children, and 15 fabulous grandchildren. Prior to entering ministry, she was a teacher and central office administrator.

Dr. Joel Tiemeyer lead, senior, and founding pastor of TWBC, is a cross-fit and soccer enthusiast who enjoys adventure and traveling to exotic beaches. He has an amazing wife and two awesome sons who he loves to do life with.

chapter 9

WHERE'S THE REMOTE? I NEED TO PRESS PAUSE!

When to Listen, When to Ask, When to Respond

BY SHAYLA HALE

LET'S BE HONEST, YOU LISTENED and reacted and now you want a do-over. This isn't the first time you wished you could take it back. Believe me, I've been there too. So, how do you press pause and then use the slow-mo feature on your mind and mouth? How can you avoid the need for a do-over?

We all know the verse, *"My dear brothers, always be willing to listen and slow to speak. Do not become angry easily"* (James 1:19, ICB) but sometimes the slow part is hard. Very hard. And if you're in a habit of not slowing down, not taking time to listen, not being careful to respond correctly, you can destroy relationships and your ministry effectiveness. Your fast forward responses can have negative kingdom impact.

As a general rule, people are terrible listeners, and as a result, not so good at responding. You're distracted, presumptuous, judgemental, autobiographical, patronizing, and prideful. Proverbs 18:13 (ICB) says, *"A person who answers without listening is foolish and disgraceful."* And when your terrible listening skills hinder your ministry and impact your relationships, you look foolish and bring disgrace upon your Savior.

WHEN TO LISTEN

There is a time to listen. Actively listen. Emphatically listen. Reflectively listen.

Here's the scenario: A parent or leader starts in on you. It's not really the time or place, but you can't get out of the situation, so you need to diffuse a potential explosion. You love this person, but you're on defense, because you're being attacked. You have no idea where this came from, but there's obviously something deeper at play. How do you understand the motivation behind the attack? How do you diffuse the attack with grace? How do you affirm the value of the person? How do you avoid an all-out argument?

Paul, late in his life and as a prisoner, wrote to Timothy, *"Stay away from foolish and stupid arguments. You know that such arguments grow into bigger arguments. And a servant of the Lord must not quarrel! He must be kind to everyone. He must be a good teacher. He must be patient. The Lord's servant must gently teach those who do not agree with him. Maybe God will let them change their hearts so that they can accept the truth"* (2 Timothy 2:23-25, ICB). When you slow down to listen you build respect, mutual understanding, empathy, and courage. You give an accuser an opportunity to have a change of heart in his attitude toward you. However, poor listening and a hasty reaction leads to judgment, disrespect, insensitivity, and dismissiveness.

Maybe you initiated the difficult conversation with a ministry volunteer, a staff member, or a parent. You know it will be uncomfortable, but it's necessary. Wouldn't it be great if all of our conversations could be easy, *"A wise person pays attention to correction that will improve his life"* (Proverbs 15:31). You want to be wise as you listen. There may be correction that can improve your life.

So, when the verbal attack comes or it's time for the difficult conversation, press pause. Take a breath. Get prepared to give focused mental energy to listening to what is being said. Don't jump to conclusions too quickly. Don't pass judgement in the moment. Be fully present with the one you're listening to without formulating a response. Absorb the accusations. You will need to sort them out later and discern the kernels of truth. Delay sharing solutions and insights for a time. Use reflection of feelings in words as you actively listen. A Native American Proverb says it well, "Listen, or your tongue will make you deaf."

"Most people do not listen with the intent to understand; they listen with the intent to reply." (Stephen R. Covey) The truth is, what you say in the moment is less important than what you enable the other person to tell you. You will have greater influence with people if you truly understand them first. Listen to their story. Avoid autobiographical listening that probes, evaluates, advises, and interprets—all from your point of view. Avoid solving the problem at this point. Just listen.

Remember, you have some time. You pressed pause.

Be aware of the signals that you need to listen up. STOP talking and listen when emotions are high, when you need to get to the heart of an issue, when you feel you don't understand, or when the other person doesn't feel understood. SLOW down and be ready to listen with empathy. GO forward with conversation when emotions are calm, when the issue is clear and understood, and when you are asked to give advice. (*The 7 Habits of Highly Effective People*, Stephen R. Covey)

Remember, slow down. Give focus to your intent to listen. Don't let little things distract you. Be aware of your non-verbal cues. Don't worry about having the correct response, and don't be afraid of silence.

Listening well takes practice. Lots and lots of practice.

WHEN TO ASK

"The first person to tell his side of a story seems right. But that may change when somebody comes and asks him questions" (Proverbs 18:17). Now it is time to press the slow-motion button. It's time to ask some questions.

Take a minute to think about how it feels when someone doesn't listen to you. How does it impact your relationship when you already have an answer before you've fully heard the situation? Often you listen with the intent to reply. You confront and offend. Or, you don't speak up at all.

After you've listened with the intent to understand, be ready to reflect back and use clarifying questions strategically. Focus on the person's story; this is not your autobiography. Reflect the emotions you heard—"It sounds like you feel sad, angry, misunderstood, unsure, frustrated, embarrassed, etc." And then ask a clarifying question—"What does that mean? Can you help me understand? Can you tell me more? What does it look like? What are you most frustrated about? What are you most angry about? What are you most worried about?"

Clarifying questions that are well formulated help you understand the person and situation you're dealing with. Those same questions can help the person better understand themself. You want to *"be slow to speak"* (James 1:19, ICB). But just like the Psalmist, you want to be understood. *"Lord, listen to my words. Understand what I am thinking"* (Psalm 5:1, ICB).

There is also wisdom in asking permission to dig a little deeper into the discussion. Sometimes people just need to be heard and they have no desire to talk with you. They want to talk at you. Empathic listening will most often open the door to clarifying questions. However, in the midst of your listening, ask the Holy Spirit to give you wisdom in what to do and say next. James 1:5 is a reminder, *"But if any of you needs wisdom, you should ask God for it. God is generous. He enjoys giving to all people, so God will give you wisdom"* (ICB).

Carefully ask the right questions, with the right attitude, at the right time.

WHEN TO RESPOND

"A wise person is known for his understanding. He wins people to his side with pleasant words" (Proverbs 16:21, ICB).

Often, in the heat of the moment, you react. And then you wish you could take it back. What you want to do instead is to respond. But, a respectful, wise response takes some time to develop. The slow motion button is still engaged.

Before formulating your response, step back and HALT—take time to consider if you are **H**ungry, **A**ngry, **L**onely, or **T**ired. You don't want emotional weakness to create an emotional response to your situation. Wait to respond if you're not at a healthy emotional place.

Proverbs reminds us, *"A gentle answer will calm a person's anger. But an unkind answer will cause more anger"* (Proverbs 15:1, ICB). Part of effective communication is seeking to be understood, much like the process of seeking to understand. You need to share your point of view, respectfully and transparently. You don't want to avoid conflict by not speaking truth, but you should *"Be kind and loving to each other. Forgive each other just as God forgave you in Christ"* (Ephesians 4:32, ICB).

As you respond, state your point of view using "I" statements. You may even try something like, "Thank you for sharing your thoughts. Would you be willing to hear mine? or "Would you be willing to listen to me like I've listened to you?" Also, be prepared to respond gently if you're interrupted—"I appreciate your thoughts. Will you be willing to hear me out before coming up with an answer?" If the conversation becomes emotional, return to active, empathic listening before you continue speaking, or take a break and come back to the conversation at a later time. You may even need to follow up with a written point of view or agree to schedule a future time to finish the conversation.

So how do you prepare a response? First, take your time ... remember, slow-mo. Clearly define the outcome you desire from your interaction: What do you want to happen as a result of your response? Consider the level of trust in the relationship. High trust and a deep connection gives you more room to work on a solution, but low trust means you will have to be very careful in your approach. Be clear about your intent for a resolution, and don't leave the interpretation of your motives to chance.

Consider how your doctor comes to a diagnosis. She needs to listen carefully to you, she asks questions to further help her understanding of the issue, and then she prescribes a treatment plan. Your doctor is careful to diagnose before she writes the prescription; to prescribe before diagnosis is foolish and dangerous. Be careful not to fall into the trap of prescribing a response before you fully diagnose the issue.

During the response, if emotions heighten, press pause and start again with empathic listening and reflecting. You are not in this to be right, to make your point, or tell them what for. You're looking to honor the Lord with a loving, gentle, response that will preserve your relationship and provide a solution that's acceptable to all. You're thinking long term—what's best for the Kingdom, your ministry, and your relationship.

You may be thinking, "What if the person really does have bad intentions, is a bully, and just wants their way?" That certainly can be the case. First, be cautious about rewarding bad behavior. If you give up to avoid the hassle, you end up teaching a lesson that behaving badly pays off ... and, it likely will happen again. Second, be careful not to play their game. Your reaction will affect your reputation; focus on your objective and keep moving toward it. Third, seek to understand, specifically their actions and intentions. Understanding their logic may help you persuade them that another approach makes sense. (*Difficult Conversations: How to Discuss What Matters Most*, Stone, Patton & Heen)

Some people really are more difficult than others. So, what happens when you can't agree? You may have to agree to disagree in a God-honoring way. Sometimes a solution cannot be agreed upon and you simply must *"Try to live in peace with all people"* (Hebrews 12:14a, ICB).

A few thoughts about where and when these conversations should take place. When you're cornered in the hall and it's getting busy, try to move to a less conspicuous location. However, it's not wise to go behind closed doors with a member of the opposite sex. Always think about integrity and how to protect yours with smart choices. When it's the third time for a conversation with this person (whether they initiate or you do) and you know the conversation is going to be difficult, you may need a third party present so there will be no misunderstandings or "he said/she said." And, you don't need to feel that you have to come to a conclusion on every conversation in the moment. When a quick conclusion is possible and you're able to listen and respond well, that's great. However, in ministry you're often caught in the hall while headed to clean up an overflowing toilet, or on your way to grab some more markers for a class, or to find a parent because a kid just bonked his head. In those situations, ask for a time to meet so you can give your full attention to the matter at hand.

Ministry is hard and wonderful all at the same time. You need to know when to listen, when to ask, and when to respond. Listening to understand, asking the right questions, and responding in love gives you the opportunity to hit the play button again. Get your remote ready. It's likely you will need it very soon.

Shayla Hale is the Minister of Family Development at Ridgecrest Baptist Church in Springfield, MO. She has pedaled across Missouri on the Katy Trail, hiked part of the Appalachian Trail, and loves to travel the beautiful world God created.

chapter 10

TALES OF CAVE DWELLERS, CAR SELLERS, AND TRUTH TELLERS

Important relationships for kidmin leaders

BY PAT CONNER

O N A SWELTERING HOT JUNE MORNING, I drove to my office feeling completely overwhelmed. So much to do! VBS was coming and there were volunteers to train, craft supplies to purchase, plans to develop, decorations and name tags and signs—oh my! Plus registration was down. Camp was scheduled on the heels of VBS. Should I do something to boost camp registration? Had the transportation been confirmed? What about camp t-shirts? Then there would be promotion with volunteers to enlist and train and new classes to form. I love my church, but why, oh why does the budgeting process have to be in high gear in June? By the time I arrived at the church offices, I was convinced. I was a miserable failure. VBS would absolutely fail. I could not get everything done. I was partly right.

As I entered the building, I was greeted with a happy hello from a favorite volunteer. She was there to help us get ready for VBS. She had brought homemade cookies. Her friends would be coming too. Things began to look a little better. The rest of the team came in and got busy. Each person was happily doing their job, encouraging every other person. There was lots of work to be done, but there was also lots of laughter and sharing and cheering and snacking. The day was fun! VBS would be great! I was not a failure at all, but I was right about the rest. I could not get everything done. I needed help.

God never intended for you to get everything done on your own. So many of His plans involve your living and working in relationships with others. When you lose sight of this, you dig a deep hole for yourself.

That's what happened to Elijah. He felt afraid, alone, and overwhelmed. What was his response? He hid in a cave. I can picture him there. Can you? He was tired and lonely. The work God had given him was too hard and it was all up to Elijah. There was no one to help him. The truth is that Elijah was pouting. God didn't let him get away with it.

1 Kings 19 tells the story of Elijah dwelling in his cave. He spent the night there, but there's no hiding from God. The word of the Lord came to him. "What are you doing, Elijah?"

Elijah responded with words something like this, "I've worked hard for you, but without results. No one cares. I'm all alone ... the only one who is doing your work." My guess is that most kidmin leaders have felt something like this. Whether most of us voice this to God is another matter. But God knows. He responded to Elijah in tender and powerful ways.

God brought Elijah into His presence, speaking to him in a soft whisper. Even that did not bring Elijah from his cave. He repeated to God his plaint, "I've worked hard for you, but without results. No one cares. I'm all alone, the only one who is doing your work." In the following verses (1 Kings 19:15-18) God reveals that there is hope for Elijah. First, God directs Elijah to anoint Elisha as his successor. He further points out to the prophet that he's not alone at all. There are 7,000 fellow believers in the land. Strengthened by the knowledge that God has prepared partners in ministry for him, Elijah leaves the cave.

You're not that different from Elijah. When things don't go as you hoped, it's easy for you to feel abandoned and hopeless. You're never abandoned! However, I'm convinced you need to train yourself to develop the relationships that will equip you to partner with others in ministry. How does this happen?

Let's look at some broad categories of relationships every kidmin leader needs.

MINISTRY RELATIONSHIPS

On the day of my pre-VBS pity party, volunteers and fellow staff members rescued me. These are people who share my passion for ministry and are willing to walk with me. There is joy in the work when we tackle it together. The mountain of work doesn't change. The deadlines don't change. The obstacles don't change. So what makes things seem different?

Part of it comes from a history of working together. We've developed trust in each other, even though there are times I might have sabotaged that process. I have days when I would rather do jobs myself than share the load. Why is that? Frankly, some of it probably is that I want things done a certain way—MY way. On the flip side, there are also days when I want to spare team members some of the work. This "Lone Ranger" mentality that communicates I will just do it myself is not right. It robs team members of being used by God. It robs all of us of the chance to grow as a team. Shared effort leads to shared accomplishment and shared joy. Each person contributes. This is how trust is built. Let's not rob our volunteers of the chance to contribute. Let's not rob ourselves of the team God has given us.

There are other important ministry relationships. Do you stop to evaluate your relationships with leaders of other ministries in your church? Does the worship leader make you crazy? Is there an underlying competition between you and the student ministry leaders? Joy and effectiveness are increased when you align your ministry and your heart with other leaders in your church. Philippians 2:3 tells us to *"consider others as more important than ourselves"* and is followed by *"Everyone should look out not only for his own interests, but also for the interests of others"* (Philippians 2:4, CSB). Though you often rightly think of this concept in terms of individuals, what if you began to think of it in terms of ministries? What if the kids' ministry team made themselves available to the student ministry team when it's time for youth camp prep? What if you brought snacks for the praise team during a late rehearsal? Maybe a few acts of thoughtfulness will open the door to stronger relationships and more effective ministry partnership.

What about that lead pastor? Does the thought of him make you tense? Or is he a strong supporter of your ministry? Is he for you or against you? Maybe the more important question to ask is this: are you for or against him? Do you support him consistently, publicly, and privately? You need him, and he needs you. The burden to position yourself to be in right relationship with him falls on you. No matter the size of your church, the lead pastor carries a heavy burden of responsibility. Are you praying for him? Do you encourage him? Do you look for ways to serve him? Do you keep him updated on your ministry? Are you earning his trust? Instead of complaining if he doesn't support you, take the responsibility to meet him more than halfway. Develop a relationship with your lead pastor on his terms.

No ministry relationships are more important than the relationships with those you are called to minister to. The kids! Do you know them by name? Do you make it a point to have conversations with them? They need you to care about them,

TALES OF CAVE DWELLERS, CAR SELLERS, AND TRUTH TELLERS

to know what's important to them, to know whats scary to them, to know about their families and their schools. If the details of executing ministry for kids gets in the way of actual personal ministry to kids, something is off. Work on developing questions and conversation starters for the kids in your ministry. Once you get past the "Who's in your family?" and "What grade are you in?" questions, move on to "What's the best thing that happened to you this week?" and "If you had three wishes, what would they be?" type questions. This will give insight that leads to relationship. A kidmin leader who doesn't know kids is missing out on real ministry.

COMMUNITY RELATIONSHIPS

Maybe you live in the heart of a huge city. Maybe you live in a wide open rural area. Wherever God has placed you, there are relationships to be developed in your community.

You're called to be the light of the world. As Christ-followers, it's right for you to develop relationships with those around you. The primary reason for this is to reflect Jesus to your community. A wonderful way kidmin leaders do this is through connecting with local schools. Get to know the principal of the elementary school near you. Find out if there are special projects your ministry could do to help the school. New landscaping? Teacher appreciation? Mentoring students? Commit your church and your ministry to supporting and loving staff and students. Community relationships can start here.

But have you considered that developing community relationships can make everyone a winner? These relationships can strengthen your witness and at the same time benefit your ministry.

For example, when you go to your local store and ask the owner for permission to display a sign promoting a special event, you're hopefully opening the door to extra publicity.

You're also opening the door to a relationship. Whether the store owner is a believer or not, you're representing Jesus. Jesus genuinely cares for others, and you will show that in your interactions. You build a foundation for more inter-actions. Imagine what can happen in the future. When the store owner's family encounters a health issue or other cri-sis, they will need ministry. You're in a position to minister. When you need 50 empty boxes or 1000 powdered donuts, you're in a position to ask.

Develop relationships with those in your community who can support your ministry in multiple ways. Who are those people? Look around!

Do you have a relationship with the owner/operator of your local movie theater? Do you know what happens to the pop-corn that smells so good but isn't sold? At the end of the day it can be bagged in giant bags and given (or maybe sold cheap-ly) to you! Not necessarily for your own personal use but as a snack for lots of hungry kids.

Who sells cars in your community? Think about it. Chanc-es are they have some big tents, and chances are they don't use them all the time. Further chances are you could use big tents for ministry. Outdoor Bible clubs? Special festivals? Do you have an auto dealer friend? He would love for you to use his tent!

Are food trucks popular in your community? We especial-ly love shaved ice or ice cream party trucks in our area. Who owns those trucks? Someone YOU can get to know! Someone who will probably be happy to bring the truck to you for a spe-cial event. Of course, they'll give you a reduced price because you're a friend, and because you will make sure they are visible to the families of your church. Good advertising for them and a fun treat for your kids or volunteers.

What interesting people have you met in your community? A cowboy? Wouldn't the kids love to see him demonstrate rop-ing at a Go Western event? A chemistry teacher? How fun for the kids to watch cool science experiments. A farmer? That farmer will love it when your kids make a special trip to visit the animals and have an outdoor picnic and hayride.

You get the idea, right? Make friends! You'll be glad you did.

PERSONAL RELATIONSHIPS

The relationships you develop personally will almost certainly cross lines; they will be relationships with people in your ministry and/or people in your community. As a leader, you should be especially diligent to develop specific types of relationships. Let me suggest three of those. Consider these questions.

Who is making you laugh? Ministry can be heavy. There will be days your spirit needs nothing more than a good long laugh. Do you have friendships where you're comfortable enough to let down your guard? Do you have friends who can see things the way you do and provide just the right hilarious perspective? Those are priceless friends. If you can't name yours now, ask the Lord to send you some. He would much rather you laugh than sit in a cave!

Who is stretching you? Do you want to stay just the way you are? Don't you want to keep getting better, keep learning, and keep growing? That doesn't happen in a vacuum. Is there someone in your life who challenges you or inspires you? There may be people in your ministry who do this. I've found networking with other kidmin leaders is a good way to be stretched. Find a few ministry leaders from other churches and schedule occasional lunch meetings. The exchange of ideas will be exciting for all of you. Don't stop growing! Ministry to kids deserves your very best.

Who is telling you the truth? It's often difficult for people to tell you how things really are. As a result, you can develop "blind spots", or areas in your lives or ministries that you fail to see as they really are. You need truth tellers—people who will give it to you straight. These are not the people who can't wait to tell you when they don't agree with something that was taught or when something went wrong in their child's class. The truth tellers you need are the people who love you enough to tell you when you're off on something, to tell you when something needs to be changed, or to hold you accountable in your personal life. It's up to you to nurture a relationship with a truth teller. No one needs more than a few of these friends. It takes time and commitment to develop the mutual trust truth-telling relationships require. You need someone who knows you and cares deeply about you. You need someone who expects the best and takes a positive view rather than a negative one. You need someone who will help you see things as God sees them. Who is that person for you?

Consider your life and ministry. Do you consistently strive to have personal relationships with those in your ministry? Do you work to develop relationships in your community? Do you seek out deeper relationships with a few people? Are you intentionally developing the relationships that will keep your ministry thriving and keep you out of the cave? This is God's plan for you. Don't miss it!

After 35 years of full-time professional ministry, **Pat Conner** is enjoying life as a writer and church consultant. Pat's greatest joys come from her 8 grandchildren along with her assorted granddogs, grandrabbits, and grandgoats.

chapter 11

BEARS, BOTTLES, AND A GOOD THINKING CAP

Get a handle on stress

BY STEPHANIE CHASE

EVERYONE HAS IT. Nobody wants it. You run from it. Why? It creates havoc in your life and wears you out. Some days it makes you sleep innumerable hours and other days it keeps you up all night. You gain weight, get sick, and hurt the ones you love because of it.

What is this maddening disease that's overtaking the world and more than likely you? Stress!

As a kids' minister, parent, spouse, friend, community leader, and church member, the chances of you experiencing stress are off the charts. If you're not dealing with the invisible trauma of anxiety today, you will one day. What do you do?

TAKE THE TEST

Before going any further, find out how stressed you really are. Take this simple test to determine your anxiety level. Put a check beside each number that is a problem for you.

☐ 1. Little or no exercise

☐ 2. Frequently late

☐ 3. Inability to relax

☐ 4. Lack of creativity

☐ 5. Inability to say "no"

☐ 6. Fatigue or exhaustion

☐ 7. Inability to forgive

☐ 8. Inflexible

☐ 9. Poor memory or recall

☐ 10. Misplaced items

☐ 11. Inability to relax

☐ 12. Rushing or skipping meals

☐ 13. Little social time

☐ 14. Difficulty listening

☐ 15. Perfectionism

☐ 16. Financial struggles

☐ 17. Procrastination

☐ 18. Recent major life crisis (divorce, move, job change, child to college, death)

☐ 19. Impatience

☐ 20. Problems with relationships

If you checked less than 5, your stress level is normal.

If you checked 5-10, you have a difficult lifestyle.

If you checked 10 or more, your stress is reaching dangerous levels.

If your stress is reaching dangerous levels, you're not alone. Anytime I present this test to groups of people, the majority of ordinary, good, well-meaning men and women are living the life God intended for them at dangerous levels. Countless people are overwhelmed, exhausted, and often depressed because of stress. People are searching desperately for ways to circumvent the tension and ask the common question, "How do I avoid all of this stress?"

The answer is simple. You won't. Jesus said, *"I have told you these things, so that in me you may have peace. In this world you will have trouble. But take heart! I have overcome the world"* (John 16:33, NIV).

Problems are unavoidable. Pain is inescapable. The hurried, exhausting life of today is unpreventable. We will have trouble. The question cannot be, "How do I avoid stress?" The appropriate question is "How do I handle it?"

GO ON A BEAR HUNT

Remember the chant you learned as a child ... "Going On A Bear Hunt"?

Going on a bear hunt, I'm not afraid.

Got my hat and my tennis shoes on.

What's that up ahead?

It's a great big field.

Can't go over it.

Can't go under it.

Guess we'll have to go through it.

(You pretended to swish across the imagined field of tall wheat.)

Next you faced the deep river.

You couldn't go under it.

Couldn't go over it.

You had to swim it.

After swimming the current of the ice cold pretend river, you saw a tree.

You couldn't go over it.

You couldn't go under it.

You had to climb it.

Branch by branch you climbed the fictitious tree sometimes holding on for life.

Lastly, when you thought you survived the fearful bear hunt, there it was, the deep dark cave.

Can't go over it.

Can't go under it.

Guess we'll have to go in it.

In the make-believe cave you faced the big, giant furry bear head on. You looked into his beady eyes. You touched his brown fur and, as fast as you could, you ran for your life until you made it home and jumped into your safe, warm bed.

Your life of stress is like going on a bear hunt. You can't go over it. You can't go under it. You have to swim, climb, and walk through days of tension and anxiety. The beauty is you do not walk alone. As a child of God, your Heavenly Father takes every step with you.

"Now this is what the Lord says—
the One who created you, Jacob, (place your name here)
and the One who formed you, Israel— (place your name here)
'Do not fear, for I have redeemed you;
I have called you by your name; you are Mine.
I will be with you
when you pass through the waters,
and when you pass through the rivers,
they will not overwhelm you.

You will not be scorched
when you walk through the fire,
and the flame will not burn you'" (Isaiah 43:1-2, HCSB).

God is with you in the current of struggle and pain. He is with you when the fire of fear, doubt, pressure, and expectation scorch your faith, confidence, and hope. The One who created you and loves you more than any other being, He is with you.

Not only does He walk with you, but He carries you. I remember as a child when our family was out way past my bedtime at various events or gatherings. My little legs would get so tired. My eyes felt like they weighed at least 20 pounds each. As a young child, I could not stay awake or carry myself any longer.

My daddy scooped me up in his arms. I gently placed my head on his shoulder and fell peacefully into sweet rest and slumber. I have no recollection of the rest of the night or how I got home. Each morning, though, after those long, tiring, exhausting nights, I woke up snuggled safely in my bed.

"Always remember, your heavenly father carries you.
See, the Lord God comes with strength,
and His power establishes His rule.
His reward is with Him,
and His gifts accompany Him.
He protects His flock like a shepherd;
He gathers the lambs in His arms
and carries them in the fold of His garment.
He gently leads those that are nursing"
(Isaiah 40:10, HCSB).

TAKE EVERY THOUGHT CAPTIVE

The key to handling stress and even better, surviving stress, starts in your mind. *"Take captive every thought and make it obedient to Christ"* (2 Corinthians 10:5, NIV). Determine today to make a list of God's promises. Post the list in a prominent place where you see it daily. Take a picture and save it on your phone or computer screen. Each day, hour, minute, depending on your level of stress, read the promises out loud and to yourself. When the weight of stress begins to overwhelm you, notice your thoughts. Stop the feelings immediately and speak God's truth.

- God is with me.
- God is carrying me.
- God loves me.
- In this world I will have trouble, but Jesus has overcome this world.
- Those who keep their mind on Jesus will stay in perfect peace.
- I am trusting in the Lord.
- I am not leaning on my own understanding.
- I acknowledge Jesus is in control right now. Jesus, You are making my path straight.
- God is working all things together for my good, because I am called according to His purpose.
- God is fighting my battles for me.

As you declare the promises of God, take deep breaths and smile. Jesus has overcome the world. He is with you, carrying you, fighting your battles for you.

DROP THE BOTTLE

A speaker once asked the audience for a volunteer. An eager young man quickly ran to the front of the room. The wise presenter handed the gentleman a full bottle of water and asked him to hold the container over his head for a minute. After the minute passed, the presenter asked the student to hold the bottle over his head for 30 minutes. Hesitantly, the young man agreed but after 15 minutes was extremely tired. "What if I asked him to hold the bottle for 24 hours? A month?"

the presenter asked the audience. "The weight and contents of the bottle has not changed. What's the difference?"

Holding stress and tension for a minute or two, maybe even 30 minutes may feel harmless, but if you hold a single bottle of water over your head for days, exhaustion, fatigue, pain, and frustration will set in. You will not be able to accomplish other expectations and needs in your life. The bottle will be a constant source of tension and anxiety that not only affects your lifestyle but those around you. The same is true with stress.

What do you do? Drop the bottle. *"Cast all your anxiety on him, because he cares for you"* (1 Peter 5:7, NIV). I challenge you right now. Take out a piece of paper and cast all your cares on Jesus. Tell Him your pain, struggle, and challenges. Write about those items checked on your stress test at the beginning of the chapter. Don't hold back. Jesus can handle every fear, worry, doubt, and point of anger. Give it to Him.

The hardest part of dropping the bottle is leaving it on the ground. One of the toughest lessons to learn in life and ministry is fully grasping the words of Jesus when He said, *"I am the vine; you are the branches. If you remain in me and I in you, you will bear much fruit; apart from me you can do nothing"* (John 15:5, NIV).

Did you hear that? Apart from Me you can do nothing. You may feel invincible, indestructible, like superman or woman, faster than a speeding bullet, more powerful than a locomotive, able to leap tall buildings in a single bound. The truth is ... apart from Jesus Christ and the daily abiding in Him you can't do squat! You will bear absolutely no fruit.

Friend, you must make sitting at the feet of Jesus, casting your cares on Him, and allowing the truth of His Word to penetrate your heart and mind the singular most important thing you do. If not, I guarantee, you will live a life of anxious stress, tension, and worry. You will miss all God has planned for you. Please, drop the botte and leave it at the feet of Jesus.

GET YOUR THINKING CAP ON

In the middle of making a decision as a child, my mom said to my brother or me, "Get your thinking cap on." This was our cue to stop and think before we spoke or made a decision. It was her way of reminding us to make a wise choice.

Much of stress is related to making decisions without your thinking cap. You hastily make unwise decisions that lead to a plethora of tension and anxiety in your life. The best part of being a child of God, a follower of Jesus, is that you have access to the wisdom of God and *"The foolishness of God is wiser than human wisdom"* (1 Corinthians 1:25, NIV). To handle stress, put your thinking cap on and tune in to the wisdom of God.

Let's look at the stress test and determine simple, wise steps that will give you what you need to get a grip, handle, and survive stress.

☐ 1. Little or no exercise

Walk 10 minutes 3 times per day. Find a friend to hold you accountable.

☐ 2. Frequently late

Set your clocks 10 minutes early. Establish arrival times 10 minutes prior to start time.

☐ 3. Inability to relax

Turn off all electronics. Sit in a place where you feel relaxed for 30 minutes daily. Take deep breaths. Dream. Pray. Think.

☐ 4. Lack of creativity

Discover what inspires you: books, quotes, music, art, nature. Invest time doing what enthuses and motivates you. Don't feel guilty doing what inspires you.

☐ 5. Inability to say "no"

- When someone asks you to do something, say, "Let me check my calendar" or "Let me check with my spouse."

Never say "yes" immediately when invited to engage in an event.

- Live by this motto: I will have lots of opportunities and very few assignments. Don't miss my assignments.

- Limit the number of activities your family will participate in.

- You do not have to go to or be part of every single thing. It's okay to say, "I'm sorry I have an appointment tonight." People don't have to know your appointment is taking a bath, having dinner with your family, or reading a book.

☐ 6. Fatigue or exhaustion

Go to bed. Get 8 hours of sleep each night. No excuses! We all have too much to do. Take a nap. Never say "I don't have time for a nap." You take time for what you make time for. Make rest a priority.

☐ 7. Inability to forgive

Pray for those you have not forgiven. Write a letter to the person revealing all of your feelings. Dispose of the letter. Meditate on what Jesus said on the cross, *"Father forgive them, they know not what they are doing."*

☐ 8. Inflexible

Release control. You don't have to have everything your way. Be flexible.

☐ 9. Poor memory or recall

Write things down.

☐ 10. Misplaced items

Clean out all closets, cabinets, rooms. The more you have, the more you will lose. Designate a place for everything.

☐ 11. Rushing or skipping meals

Eat dinner with your family daily. Turn off all electronics. Take your time and enjoy meals. Chew food 32 times before swallowing.

☐ 12. Little social time

Make time for people you love. Play. Laugh. Enjoy fun times with friends and family. *"A cheerful heart is good medicine"* (Proverbs 17:22, NIV). Be sure to laugh.

☐ 13. Difficulty listening

Don't interrupt. Focus on what someone is saying without thinking about what you want to say next. Practice listening to podcasts.

☐ 14. Perfectionism

Nobody is perfect except Jesus. Let it go!

☐ 15. Financial struggles

Tithe. Get out of debt. Follow the Dave Ramsey plan.

☐ 16. Procrastination

Just do it. Do the hard things first.

☐ 17. Recent major life crisis (divorce, move, job change, child to college, death)

Give yourself time to grieve. See a counselor.

☐ 18. Impatience

Imagine what someone else is going through. You never know!

☐ 19. Problems with relationships

Take a personality test. Learn your strengths and weaknesses. Accept others. You don't have to be friends with everyone. You are the king or queen of your castle. You are the only person who releases the drawbridge to allow people into your fort. Some people need to stay outside. You can wave at a distance and be kind. Others need to be dear to your heart. Determine the difference and put your thinking cap on.

☐ 20. Being healthy

Drink water. Choose protein and veggies. Eat smaller portions.

The most challenging part of stress is that you control it. You are the only one who can limit activities, say "no", or put yourself to bed. Only you can put your thinking cap on and do the wise thing. You determine what goes in your mouth and the forgiveness you will extend to people you love. You are the only one who can cut up a credit card and stop spending your money. And most importantly, only you can cast all of your cares on Jesus, take your thoughts captive, and make them obedient to Him. Only you can drop the bottle at the master's feet and allow Him to carry you through your seasons of stress. My recommendation, do what only you can do. Get a handle on stress one small step at a time and watch Jesus turn your tension into treasured time and your anxiety into awesome moments with Him.

Stephanie Chase has been married to Rick for 25 years, is mom of 3 grown kids, and Granny to the cutest little dude ever. She loves leading kids' ministry at Champion Forest Baptist Church in Houston almost as much as eating ice cream, running, and teaching.

chapter 12

LIVING PAST THE HURT
What happens after burnout

BY JORDAN DAVIS

L ET'S BE OPEN AND HONEST from the start. Sometimes church life stinks! In all honesty, church people can be some of the hardest people you will ever deal with. I'll never forget sitting across the desk from my senior pastor hearing a list of everything I had ever done wrong. For those two years I had worked and fashioned a ministry I was proud of, and then seemingly out of the blue, I was read a laundry list of mishaps, misconceptions, and misrepresentations that had never been brought up before. This isn't to say that the pastor himself is a bad person, but sometimes church people are just that ... people, who also make mistakes and handle things the best they can in the moment.

Sitting here years later I can openly admit that I had a hand in the situation. I pushed a little hard, changed a little too much, too fast, and was not clear in my direction. Most importantly, I didn't allow time for my ministry volunteers to buy-in to "my" vision. After I resigned from that children's ministry job I realized how, aside from loosing my position, I was also burned out.

What happened to me was easily avoidable. I just made some crucial mistakes. Before you can dive into how to get over burnout, you must look at what throws you into this vicious cycle. There are some rather simple fixes that will help you avoid the cycle, and most importantly avoid burnout.

PUSHING CHANGE!

One of the biggest reasons people fall into the trap of hurt and burnout is that they're not getting "their way." You begin with great intentions to bring change to a ministry. You bring a fresh vision of moving forward, you start pressing issues, maybe starting small, but once you gain momentum, many times you push harder. Then, there are the occasional times where you push just a little too hard. You justify it by knowing you may have many people on your side. But most of the time, "sides" have no positive outlook when it's inside the walls of the church. (That's a Jesus thing you know ... no divisions in the Church.) When you get the inevitable pushback, you feel it's a personal attack or vendetta on you, and that causes hurt.

The answer: relax. Remember, ministry is a marathon and not a sprint. Change takes time, and if it's something that's beneficial and right for your ministry, then the change will be naturally adapted.

NOT BEING FED!

One of the scariest days I ever had in ministry was in the midst of a mentoring call I had. I was listening to my mentor ask me many questions in which I was able to fire off quick answers. Until suddenly, he asked me when the last time was that I, as a children's pastor, sat in church for a full service. I had to stop and think about it for a minute. My answer hit us both like a ton of bricks. It had been over two years since I'd found a seat in our sanctuary to worship and listen to a message. He then asked me what I was doing to change the situation. I fed him a bunch of excuses, followed by me honestly admitting that I was going to do ... nothing!

The answer: I realized I would always have an excuse until I made church service attendance a top priority on my "to-do" list. So, what I began doing is a bit unconventional. I started attending a different church on Saturday nights so that I could still run the ministry on Sunday mornings. I know that may be a hard pill to swallow for some people reading this, but your church is not the only place you can be fed. Unfortunately, in the position I was in, and the position my church was in, I needed to be around on Sunday mornings.

I found incredible freedom in going to a different church. How does this sound: Getting to walk into a church building not worrying if the nursery was staffed, not checking your phone on the way in to see multiple cancelations from volunteers, or better yet, not needing to make that last minute stop to buy goldfish, shaving cream, and plungers. Dream with me: walking into a church service, leaving your phone in the car, entering worship distraction free. That's freedom.

Maybe you don't have the ability to go to a different church, but I really do challenge you to find freedom in worship. That may be in a place, a moment, an attitude. Find your Sabbath and create the space for connection with God. If you aren't being fed yourself, you will have nothing to pour out for your ministry. Your cup must runneth over.

FEELING ALONE!

Ministry can be one of the loneliest occupations. You use so much caution when it comes to making friends and trusting people. You're on call 24/7 and hear everything about people's lives. It's hard to speak God's truth into people who get offended when you say that change is needed, or when you challenge people to grow. This feels especially true when you deem those same people "friends", and then see how loose they use that term when they stop coming to your church or supporting the ministry that they "used to love."

The answer: Seek counseling for yourself and seek accountability with other leaders in your area. Schedule a lunch each week that's not a working lunch, but one that is a mental wellness lunch. This means when you're meeting with a pastor or leader in your organization do not talk about work or anything associated with it. I bet that's harder than you think.

LACK OF DIRECTION

Sometimes, one of the hardest realities to accept is that your actions are just not worth following. I'm not saying anything about morals or sinful actions ... those are obviously actions not worth following. What I'm saying is that sometimes we just plain make poor decisions. Others know it, others see it, and others feel it. A lack of direction leads to frustration. Where are you heading? Where is your ministry heading? Where is your team supposed to aim? If you can't answer those questions, then you can be certain that your lack of direction is hurting your ministry.

The answer: Create a team that knows your heart and shares your vision. You need a team that you can bounce ideas off of. You need a team you can trust for feedback. Don't just offer them space to talk, but really hear their hearts as part of the leadership. What you'll realize is that some of your ideas may not be as good as you thought they were. Explain those ideas to your team (or try to explain ... ya know, like how to shove that watermelon in a shoe to do a relay race). A team could be as small as one other person, but it's someone who shares your vision and knows your direction.

NOT BEING TEACHABLE/COACHABLE

Oy, did he just go there? Yes! Burnout can happen when you're not allowing someone else to pour into you. When you get to a moment when you think you're done learning, you will fail. If you have an "I've done it all and I've learned it all" attitude, you're in a very dangerous spot.

The answer: As a leader, you have to constantly be learning. You can learn by observing others. You'll notice things to do or not to do. You can learn by your own trial and error. Learn by doing. Try something new. There are so many great avenues to expand your own knowledge. Just search the web for some great new ideas. I'm sure someone has tried it already.

I would also say that just as important as being coachable yourself, you need to continue the cycle and be on the lookout for someone to coach. Be coached and, in turn, coach someone else.

GET OVER IT.

Whew! Getting past the hurt of burnout is so very hard and honestly it sometimes can feel like you may never fully get past it. Sometimes in your burnout you feel an entire gamut of emotions like grief, anger, depression, fear, and so many more. And then there is the rebound—the moment you feel like you're ready to jump back into ministry but start having second thoughts or hesitations.

Here are just a few ways you can begin to get over the hurt and burnout associated with ministry.

Remove yourself from all ministry jobs. This could be a sabbatical if your ministry participates in that, or just requesting a time for refreshing and renewal. You need time to heal and you have to start within. Relinquishing control of the ministry, even if you're just volunteering, while you're healing from burnout is one of your very first steps.

Seek wise council. Honestly, I wish someone had insisted that I seek counseling while I was in ministry. This is just one step you can take to work through some of the irrational thoughts and decisions that plague ministers. Give yourself the space to speak openly with someone who is an unbiased party, someone who gives you permission to say the things you only wish you could say.

Find your identity. So often, you suffer from "mistaken identity" when you're in the trenches of ministry. You "go and do" ministry for years and finally, when you slow down or change courses, you look in the mirror and feel like you've failed. You feel like you failed those who spoke life into you. You feel like you failed those who honored your call. You feel like you failed those you've previously served, all because you're no longer doing ministry. But that's not the case. The real issue is that you sought your identity in ministry and not in Jesus Christ. Foremost, you are a son or daughter of the King!

Know what matters most. When you're burned out as a leader, it doesn't just effect you. It effects those closest to you. If you have a family, know that they matter most and they often suffer alongside you. Date your spouse, train your children to be godly and not just good, and pour into those relationships that are timeless.

Forgive yourself. This may be a newsflash, but you're not perfect, so quit acting as if you are. Grace saved you, and grace will continue working in your life. Where you are now—the pit you feel like you're in—is not a life sentence, and certainly does not surprise God to see you in this place. God will never lead you to a place and abandon you. He is just waiting for you to rest and wait for Him. Learn from your past and press into God for your future.

There is life on the other side of burnout. You can get through this season in your life and you can be better because of it. Burnout may change who you are and the way you look at ministry, but it does not have to be the end all of your ministry journey. Look with new, expectant eyes at the future and allow this season to shape you. You can live in hurt and burnout or you can learn and grow through it to be the best you that you can be.

Jordan Davis is a fun-loving, big guy, in a kids' world. He loves seeing kids grow into their own personal knowledge and understanding of a relationship with Jesus. Along with his wife, Kati, they are raising 3 young boys to be great men of God and leaders in the Kingdom.

chapter 13

KNOWING, GROWING, AND SOWING LEADERS

The difference between equipping and developing leaders

BY TRISH WEEKS

THINK BACK TO YOUR FAVORITE TEACHER. What do you remember? They might have been especially kind, or inspiring, or funny. Maybe they explained things in a way you could understand. Whatever it was that made them your favorite, I'm betting it was based on the way they related to you.

The same is true about any connection you have with someone else. Christianity is about relationship. Family is about relationship. Friendship is about relationship. And leadership is about relationship.

RELATIONSHIPS

You know the adage to be true: people don't care how much you know until they know how much you care. Every step in the volunteer pipeline from recruiting, to training, to equipping and developing leaders relies on relationships. However, not all relationships are the same.

Your relationships vary based upon how much you're around and how invested you are in an individual. In your life you know many people and probably have several friends, but only a few close friends. In much the same way, you must also consider and apply this relationship dynamic to your ministry.

According to John Maxwell, leadership is influence. Since kids' ministry usually requires a large volunteer base, you lead and influence many people, but the affect and degree of influence is directly proportional to the level of your relationship with them. While your impact reaches numerous people, your day-to-day interactions are comprised of a smaller, select group. It must and should be this way. I categorize these groups of people as those you know, those you grow, and those you sow.

Those you KNOW: Volunteers you Lead

Those you GROW: Volunteers you Equip

Those you SOW: Volunteers you Develop

EQUIPPING VS. DEVELOPING

Building a sustainable ministry team requires you lead many and that you intentionally invest time and energy in equipping and developing a few that will, in turn, help you lead others. At first glance, it may seem that equipping and developing are synonymous, and that talking about the difference between them is just semantics. A few years ago, this is what I believed as well. It was a vague concept, because I didn't understand the differences, but this insight brought growth and transformation to me and my team.

The reality is that the difference between equipping and developing leaders is the difference between training and transforming, between giving answers and asking questions, between adding and multiplying. It is the difference between the idea that people do the work and people are the work. It is the difference between believing people help us accomplish the mission and believing that people are the mission.

Equipping focuses on improving skills, managing things and tasks, and is concentrated on the project or product. It's about training people to help do the work of ministry. It focuses on the "what" and "how." Developing focuses on seeing the value in a person and communicating it in a way that they are inspired to see it themselves. It concentrates on what lies within the person and encourages and empowers them to rise to their full potential. It focuses on the "who" and "why."

In an article titled "The Best Long Term Strategy for Church Growth", Dan Reiland lays out the differences this way:

Equipping is the process of training a person for a specific ministry.
Developing is the process of investing in a person for their personal growth.

Equipping is focused on the church's agenda.
Developing is focused on the person's agenda.

Equipping is an exchange based on transaction.
Developing is essentially a gift that contributes to transformation.

Another way to look at it is that equipping people maximizes their abilities. It helps them to be better able to do the work they are called to do in the areas in which they serve. Developing maximizes the leadership abilities of a few to maximize the abilities of many. It also helps prepare them to step into new ministry opportunities that God calls them to do.

Once you understand the difference between equipping and developing, you need to ask yourself, "Which leaders should I be equipping and which leaders should I be developing?" Both are an integral part of leadership development, but there are different levels of investment you need to make for a leadership culture to be effective.

One of my mentors says energy is the number one resource you must learn to steward. You only have a given amount of time and energy and you must decide how, where, and when that energy is invested. The more invested you are in someone, the deeper the relationship. This is where you make the distinction between the relationships of knowing, growing, and sowing.

KNOW – THOSE YOU LEAD

Regardless of the size of your church or department, you know many people, and many people know you! You have influence over all the volunteers you lead in your ministry when you cast vision, develop policies and procedures, and establish a positive environment in which they serve along with a culture in which they grow.

However, your relationship with them might be confined to a handshake and a smile. You're friendly and can call them by name, maybe know a little about them and their family, but your association with them is based on them serving in your department. Due to the volume of volunteers needed in a kids' ministry, your relationship with them is limited and so is your ability to personally equip and develop them.

GROW – THOSE YOU EQUIP

It's your job to move volunteers from a place of serving to a place of growing. One way you do that is to make sure volunteers are equipped. They need training in their specific roles and duties. Expectations, policies, and procedures should be clear. To have a ministry that runs well and meets the needs of the people it serves, volunteers need to know what they are to do and how they are to do it. No one wants to be put in a position and fail. They want to know what's expected. This is equipping. Depending on the volunteer base, this training might be done by you directly, but the reality is you have many classrooms and areas you lead. Kids' ministry includes a variety of environments and ages, each one having specific goals and purposes.

Consider all the different training that needs to happen from greeters to check-in, from hall monitors to teachers, from nursery to toddlers, from preschool to elementary, from changing diapers to worship, from calming a child to correcting a child, from snack to bathroom breaks, from safety to technology. There are numerous details regarding engaging kids and families that can't be overlooked, and they vary depending on where the volunteer is serving.

It would be exhausting and impossible for you to train every volunteer in each of these responsibilities! One of the best ways I've found to train volunteers is to develop a leadership team and have veterans train and mentor the new recruits. A simple idea of what this looks like from the mentor's viewpoint is:

I do; You watch.

I do; You help.

You do; I help.

You do, I watch.

You do ... and train someone else!

As they mature, you help them grow by providing continual opportunities for them to discover and use their gifts and talents.

SOW – THOSE YOU DEVELOP

Using a leadership team to grow and equip volunteers allows you to steward your own time and energy to sow into and develop your top leaders. Developing focuses on investing in and leading people by placing greater value on who they are as a person rather than what they do. In this relationship, you have the greatest impact and influence as you see the gifts, talents, and potential in someone, and recognize their worth is based on more than their work. It empowers them to embrace new challenges and ministries that God places on their heart. Lasting change comes when you make someone better, not something better.

The beloved Mr. Fred Rogers said it this way, "As human beings, our job in life is to help people realize how rare and valuable each one of us really is, that each of us has something that no one else has—or ever will have—something inside that is unique to all time. It's our job to encourage each other to discover that uniqueness and to provide ways of developing its expression."

The key to making the mentor relationship work is relationship. It does take time and energy but this leadership paradigm maximizes your effectiveness as you develop leaders who equip others. John Maxwell says you teach what you know, but you reproduce who you are.

Stephen Covey, in his book *7 Habits of Highly Effective People,* says that leadership is primarily a function of who you are, for this is the foundation for everything you do. He calls it living from the inside out and that you should purpose to share what you've learned with someone else within the first 48 hours of learning it.

What a great approach to developing others! You intentionally sow into a few who then sow into others. This ministry model has the unique potential to reproduce itself.

LADDER HOLDERS

You might call this small group of key leaders your inner circle or executive team. Dr. Sam Chand calls them "Ladder Holders" in his books *Who's Holding Your Ladder* and *Ladder*

Holders. Dr. Chand says that you can do it all yourself which is too much work; you can hire it out which is too much money; or you can develop others which takes time, but in the end is the most productive and sustainable. He goes on to say that your success as a leader is not dependent on your ladder climbing skills but rather is contingent on who is holding your ladder.

The leaders who are in your inner circle are those you trust and value, and they are your closest relationships since much of your time and energy is invested in them. As you sow into these ladder holders and develop them, they in turn equip others. *"And the things you have heard me say in the presence of many witnesses entrust to reliable people who will also be qualified to teach others"* (2 Timothy 2:2, NIV).

HELPING OTHERS FULFILL THEIR CALL

"So Christ himself gave the apostles, the prophets, the evangelists, the pastors and teachers, to equip his people for works of service, so that the body of Christ may be built up until we all reach unity in the faith and in the knowledge of the Son of God and become mature, attaining to the whole measure of the fullness of Christ. Then we will no longer be infants, tossed back and forth by the waves, and blown here and there by every wind of teaching and by the cunning and craftiness of people in their deceitful scheming. Instead, speaking the truth in love, we will grow to become in every respect the mature body of him who is the head, that is, Christ. From him the whole body, joined and held together by every supporting ligament, grows and builds itself up in love, as each part does its work" (Ephesians 4: 11-16, NIV).

Each person, working together, using their gifts and in the relationships of equipping, as well as developing, builds up the body of Christ. In regards to Ephesians 4, Dan Reiland says, "Equipping works best in an environment where the people do not see their service as 'helping the pastor get his work done.' Ephesians 4 makes it clear that the pastor is helping people fulfill their call to serve others and build up the body of Christ." He goes on to define the difference between equipping and developing. "Equipping prepares people to *do* ministry; developing builds up the people who are *in* ministry. Equipping changes the ministry. Developing changes the person." (*Amplified Leadership*, Dan Reiland)

EQUIPPING AND DEVELOPING

While equipping and developing are different, both are needed in the church for unity and maturity. It's important to train people to do what they need to do and how to do it. It's also important to add value to the person so they do it better.

I saw one acronym for TEAM as Together Everyone Achieves More. Everyone wants to be part of the team, to see their value, and to be in their place. As the leader, your influence impacts all the layers of leadership in your ministry—those you know, grow, and sow into. The relationships you have with your ladder holders and the relationships they have with those they are equipping strengthen the ministry as a whole.

The true worth of ministry is not found in developing your individual gifts but in developing the gifts of those around you. Leadership is creating an environment that values people and provides opportunities for them to grow. In the safety of relationship, leadership is taught and caught.

John Maxwell says there is no such thing as a full-grown tree. You must continually grow yourself and invest in the equipping and developing of the leaders in your ministry, even when the relationships that define them can be messy and take time and energy. But what is the alternative? I'll leave you with this thought: A leader was asked, "What if we spend the time to equip and develop people and they leave?" The leader answered, "What if we don't and they stay?"

Trish Weeks is the former children's pastor at Tree of Life Church in New Braunfels, TX. Most kidmin do not hold a third-degree black belt in karate, but Trish does ... and it comes in handy sometimes!

chapter 14

WHEN NO ONE ELSE IS WEARING SKINNY JEANS

Leading a generation older than you

BY JULIA BALL

WHEN I STARTED MY FIRST full-time ministry position 4 1/2 years ago, I was barely 21. I was newly married and had my freshly framed university diploma hanging on my office wall. My bookshelves were filled with the latest theology and leadership books. My brain was full of ideas galore—how I would direct my ministries, impact my church, dazzle them with my intelligence, and change the world (all within my first six months there, of course).

My naive idealism quickly got a reality check when I looked around the congregation my husband and I had joined and realized that 99% of them were older than me, had been serving Jesus longer than me, and brought much more life experience and wisdom to the table. Some of them had been teaching Sunday school for longer than I'd been alive!

As a Bible college student, I pictured myself leading a vibrant team of teenage and young adult volunteers who wanted to be just like me! I imagined myself pouring the wisdom I'd gleaned during my time at university into them. They would want to go out for lunch and ice cream and coffee. I would be the leader of a dynamic team of millennials. We would impact the children we ministered to, one skinny-jean wearing, latte-drinking, Spotify-streaming leader at a time.

You can imagine then, how, when I looked out over that congregation—with millennials few and far between—my confident "I got this!" turned into a "What in the world do I have to offer these people?" followed with a "How am I going to get them to volunteer?" I felt overwhelmed with the task at hand. In all my training up to that point, nobody had ever mentioned that as a children's pastor, I would have to lead people who were older, wiser, and more mature than I was. Where was I going to go from here?

Thankfully, with the mentorship of a great lead pastor, a lot of prayer, vision-casting and hard work, I've moved out of that place of disillusionment and confusion. Today, I am blessed with an incredible team of volunteers (who are practically all older than me) that I love and respect. They look to me for leadership, and I can count on them to impact the lives of kids. They may not wear skinny jeans or even know what Spotify is, but they are changing the next generation, one child at a time.

So, how did I get there? How can children's pastors, especially those of us who are younger, lead those older than us, and more importantly, lead them well? In the next few pages, I'd like to share with you my own journey towards leading an older generation, and how I believe you can too!

GAIN THEIR TRUST

Anytime I'm given the opportunity to share on this topic with other children's ministry leaders, I emphasize one thing: You must gain the trust of the people you want to lead.

Before starting in a full-time staff position, most of my ministry experience had been leading kids, junior high students, or my own peers. It seemed to me, for some reason, trust came more quickly when I was leading people around my own age or younger. Junior high students automatically listened to what I had to say (well, as much as junior high students listen to anyone) when I was wearing a t-shirt or name tag that identified me as a leader.

The older generation, while they treated me with the utmost respect, wasn't automatically going to trust me because I had "Pastor" in front of my name on my door or in the bulletin. I had to gain their trust, and this wasn't a process that happened overnight.

In order to gain the trust of those people I wanted to come alongside me, I had to prove to them I was a leader worth following. I had to display to them that I was trustworthy, that I lived with integrity, and that I wasn't out to turn their church upside down.

For me, and I'm willing to bet for you too, this didn't ... and won't ... require some grand gesture or demonstration. I gained the trust of the people in my church family by consistently showing up. I showed up on Sundays, wearing dress pants instead of ripped jeans, because I wanted them to see they could take me seriously. When I was given the opportunity to lead worship, I mingled familiar songs they had been singing for years with newer ones I wanted to introduce. I wanted them to see, even through my worship leading, that I was here to make changes by building on what was already present, not by tearing it down.

I was reliable. I showed up on time (well, mostly). I tried not to rock the proverbial boat. I listened to what they had to say, and showed them even though I was young, I cared about them and wanted them to trust me.

Here's the truth: Nobody is going to follow a leader they can't trust. And while you may be the most trustworthy person on the planet, the people in your congregation won't know that unless you show them. So, be reliable. Be humble. And show them, one small step at a time, that they can trust you.

GET TO KNOW THEM

As I worked to gain the trust of the people in my congregation, I also worked on another task—getting to know them. I'm blessed to be part of a smaller church (just under 100 people), so this may have been easier for me than it is for some of you!

That being said, I'm an extreme introvert, so getting to know a congregation of 100 people felt like as great a task of getting to know 1000. After a large number of pep talks to myself in my office, I embarked on the task of getting to know the people in my church family.

Getting to know them didn't mean that I learned the intimate details of every single life. But, I did work at matching names to faces. I worked at asking simple questions: Do you have any grandkids? Where do you work? What have you done since you retired? How long have you attended this church?

I wanted people to know that I didn't just see them as potential volunteers. I wanted them to know that I genuinely cared about them, their families, and their stories whether or not they chose to volunteer in the ministries I was building.

As I got to know people, it was also an important reminder for me that ministry is about exactly that—people. While it can be easy to focus on just the kids you're teaching and leading, I'm equally as responsible to lead and care for the volunteers in my care. The same strategies I employ to get to know and invest in kids need to carry over to adults.

Hearing the stories of those who had lived much longer than me helped me appreciate them so much more. Through this process, I gained mentors and friends who are old enough to be my parents and grandparents. As I lead them, they impact me and pour into my life.

GIVE THEM A JOB THEY CAN DO

Of course, gaining trust and getting to know the people I wanted to lead didn't happen overnight. It happened over the course of months, and is still happening, over four years into this role. I am constantly reminding myself that I need to act in ways to gain and keep the trust of my church family. I can't use getting to know people as a means to an end. It must be a consistent part of my ministry and leadership.

As I got to know people in my congregation, some of them started to express interest in being part of the ministry I was growing. In my context, an active children's ministry had fallen by the wayside. There were a few committed Sunday school teachers, but numbers had dwindled and they were ready to revamp and reach the next generation.

That task seemed daunting though. Some of those who wanted to be involved in the ministry were in their 70s (or older) and the idea of jumping around to the latest Yancy tune or screaming during games seemed overwhelming.

I realized that if I wanted to lead these people, I needed to start by giving them a job they could do. This meant tweaking the methods I used in kids' ministry. Many of my early leaders were behind the scenes. They manned registration tables, cleaned up, and handed out snacks. They knew how to make crafts, so guess what? They taught kids how to make crafts instead of the cool science experiments or high-energy activities I had envisioned.

With time, they grew comfortable in these jobs. They gained confidence! They could do this! As they started to excel in these jobs, I started to push them outside of their comfort zones into new roles. I talked about the importance of small groups (in our setting, we call them "crews") and how I believed they could be a crew leader!

"Just act like you're hanging out with your grandkids!" was my infamous line. Soon enough, these gray-haired, glasses-wearing grandparents were sitting with groups of six kids, leading them through stations, praying with them, and even testing out those latest dance moves!

SELL A VISION

If I could only go back four years to my first weeks in this role, I'd tell myself that everything was going to be okay. It would be a process, but with time, I'd grow a volunteer team that respected and followed my leadership.

In case you were wondering how things have turned out, this past summer, at our Kids Xperience, I was blessed with over 40 volunteers. That's nearly half of my church family! The cool thing about that, was over half of those volunteers were older than me, and most significantly so.

As our volunteers arrived sporting their brand-new, rebranded "Staff" shirts, my heart was overwhelmed, nearly to the point of tears. These parents of teenagers, adults, and grandparents were ecstatic to be a part of what we were doing to reach the next generation. They knew the names of the kids in their crews, they gave hugs and high-5s as kids arrived and left, and they loved doing it. Seeing the smiles on the faces of children, and on the faces of their leaders, was a surreal experience for me.

As I reflect on this summer's Kids Xperience (affectionately known as KX in our church), I realize that those volunteers follow, not because I'm such an amazing leader, but because they bought into the vision I was selling. That vision isn't my own, although I wish I could take credit for it.

As I gained the trust of my congregation—getting to know people and giving them jobs—I constantly painted a picture. That picture was birthed out of 1 Timothy 2:3-4 (NLT), which reads: *"This is good and pleases God our Savior, who wants everyone to be saved and understand the truth."*

Whenever I was given an opportunity, through a post on our Facebook page, a church-wide email, a sermon, or an announcement in our Sunday service, I reiterated the vision behind these verses. Everything that I was doing in children's ministry was for one purpose—to partner with God in seeing people come into His Kingdom. I didn't want our church family, no matter how young or old, to miss out on being a part of that!

Ultimately, that's what has allowed me to lead a generation that's older than me. We've come together for one common cause—to see people come to know Jesus. While we differ in a lot of areas, when we focus on doing all we can to lead people to Jesus, we work together incredibly.

No matter what age or stage of life, Jesus-followers get excited about leading people to Christ. Children's ministry is an amazing opportunity to see that firsthand. As I've been able to paint that picture, and allow my volunteers to witness lives impacted for the Gospel, they've followed my lead.

New ideas, changes in programming, and steps outside our comfort zones (mine and theirs!) are all a part of the journey of reaching the next generation.

So, if you're blessed with a congregation that's older than you, sell them that vision. Remind them why you exist. Let them get in on the action. And I can guarantee they will follow where you lead. I can also guarantee as they follow, you will learn from them. Watching the way the older generation pours love out onto these kids is challenging to me. They're leading me to love more deeply and let each child into my heart. They remind me of how to pray for this generation, as many of them tell me they pray for each child in their group by name.

It's a beautiful thing. And while I may be the only one sporting skinny jeans, I wouldn't want it any other way.

Julia Ball is a proud mom of a rambunctious 1-year-old and wife to super pastor and dad, Andrew. She currently serves as Children's and Family Pastor in Clarenville, Newfoundland, Canada, and Provincial Children's Director for her denomination. You can find her online at ministrymom.ca.

chapter 15

SUSCEPTIBLE OR SUSTAINABLE?

How your choices guide your ministry

BY RACHAEL GROLL

I COULDN'T BELIEVE THE WORDS that had just come out of my mouth. It was a moment that I couldn't take back, that I immediately knew would have bigger consequences than I was prepared for. I had just told a well-meaning but poorly executing volunteer to leave, and that I would rather do everything myself than to have him help me. Although my reasoning for wanting him gone may have been justified, my actions were not. As I sat there alone in the room, with a classroom full of preschoolers, I realized that I was in a little over my head. It's a moment that many of you have experienced from time to time, when you feel overburdened and over stressed. Had I been well rested, with lots of extra help, I may have not reacted as poorly that day. Instead, I was overwhelmed with what I knew I should be doing instead of what I actually had to do.

Since that time, I have climbed out of that mess and have raised up a wonderful team of volunteers. However, the damage I did with that careless comment took years to repair. It didn't just cost me that one volunteer, but several others that he had close ties with. As I worked tirelessly to manage a busy children's department, there were a couple things I struggled with early on that could easily have been avoided if I had allowed others to help me. Instead, I took on the brunt of the tasks, working myself into a stressed out and overburdened mess.

As I look back at that time, there are several reasons why I was in that position, and none of them had to do with my intentions. My intentions were good. I intended to provide the best program I possibly could. I intended to be an encourager. I intended to minister to those God put in my path. I intended to make sure all my bases were covered. I intended to take a sabbath every week and to get to sleep at a decent hour. However, there was a disconnect between my intentions and my reality.

If you take a look at the early church, there are a few parallels you can see between the first century church and the programs you strive to run now. In the beginning of Acts, you see a biblical model that you often look to as the ideal way to care for one another. In Acts 2:45 (NASB) it says, *"and they began selling their property and possessions and were sharing them with all, as anyone might have need."* I want to draw attention to one small word in that verse—all. They were working tirelessly to make sure the needs of *all* were met. You see this system elaborated on a little later in Acts.

> *"All the believers were one in heart and mind. No one claimed that any of their possessions was their own, but they shared everything they had. With great power the apostles continued to testify to the resurrection of the Lord Jesus. And God's grace was so powerfully at work in them all that there were no needy persons among them. For from time to time those who*

owned land or houses sold them, brought the money from the sales and put it at the apostles' feet, and it was distributed to anyone who had need" (Acts 4:32-35, NIV).

The word says that there was "no needy persons among them." The apostles were tasked with the social mission of meeting the needs of the people with the resources that were provided to them through God's hand of provision. This was a time when the early church was growing. God blessed them and they were working hard to advance the kingdom. That sounds a lot like those of us in full-time ministry. You are called by God to meet the needs of God's people: spiritual needs, emotional needs, and physical needs. Except, there is one more piece to this puzzle that I want to draw your attention to.

"Now at this time while the disciples were increasing in number, a complaint arose on the part of the Hellenistic Jews against the native Hebrews, because their widows were being overlooked in the daily serving of food" (Acts 6:1, NASB).

Did you catch that? Widows being overlooked. How could this have happened? You just read a couple chapters earlier that the disciples were providing for *all*, and that there were *no needy persons among them*. Yet, here in chapter 6 you read that there were widows being overlooked. Who were these widows? The Bible refers to them as Hellenistic widows. At this time in Israel's history, there was already a bit of a divide in culture. You had your Hebraic Jews, who were the traditional, Hebrew speaking Jews. Then, you had your Hellenistic Jews, who were the ones who spoke Greek. Although many Hebrew Jews also spoke some Greek, they worshiped and spoke primarily Hebrew. For the Greek Jews, however, many of them were from foreign lands. The Jews believed that there was virtuous significance to being buried in Jerusalem. As a result, many foreign Jews trekked to Jerusalem to die, leaving behind a number of widows who did not have friends and family to care for them. These widows became the marginalized of society, hidden from the hands of the disciples who were supposed to be caring for them.

I'm sure there are a variety of reasons that these widows were overlooked. The Bible has a clear mandate for caring for widows, a mandate that the disciples took very seriously. But there was a disconnect between their intentions and their reality. This brings me to my first point.

1. If you fail to delegate in your ministry, someone will be overlooked, despite your intentions.

The disciples had hearts to serve God's people. They worked tirelessly to advance the Kingdom. They knew the mandate to care for widows. Yet, it wasn't until a complaint was raised that they realized their oversight. I know that often times you want to dismiss complaints. I would encourage you, despite your emotions, to consider the root of a complaint before you dismiss it. Most times, when there is a complaint, it's because of an unmet need. It would be naive of you to think that you could meet all the needs of all the people, all of the time. But are the needs you are tasked with meeting, mandated by in the Word of God, being met? Part of leadership is being open to admitting your mistakes and then fixing them. That's exactly what you see the disciples do next. They fix the problem.

"Therefore, brethren, select from among you seven men of good reputation, full of the Spirit and of wisdom, whom we may put in charge of this task. But we will devote ourselves to prayer and to the ministry of the word" (Acts 6:3-4, NASB).

As the disciples start to delegate administrative tasks to others, you realize this is necessary for you as well. You can use their model for your own process of delegation—seeking out those who are full of faith, wise, and honest, through prayer. Notice that there is not a mention of talent. So often, when you are recruiting for positions within your ministry, your first inclination can be looking for someone who is a gifted teacher, a talented artist, or an outgoing personality. The disciples started their search with prayer. It ended with character. I truly believe that a servant's heart is much more important than their skill level. As you see the transference of responsibilities take place, be encouraged by what you see as a result later in verse 7. *"The word of God kept on spreading; and the number of the disciples continued to increase greatly in Jerusalem"* (Acts 6:7, NASB). The disciples were able to increase their capacity for ministry by letting go of the things they were not called to do in exchange for focusing on what they were. Their ministry changed from being susceptible to sustainable. Yours can too.

2. Let go of the things you're doing that you're not called to do.

For me, this became a process of taking a hard look at what I wanted to do verses what I was called to do. If you're in a position of leadership within your church, there is a specific reason God has placed you there. You each have a unique role and calling within the body of Christ. You need to be free to do what you're called to do, and let go of what you're not called to do. That's easier said than done. You see how easily the disciples got distracted from their primary duty, and the burden of the work became too much. Their oversight of the widows was not deliberate. Their neglect of the needs of those who were overlooked in their culture was an inadvertent symptom of the disciples doing more than what they were called to do.

3. Who am I overlooking because I am doing things I am not called to do?

Who might the unseen, the overlooked people in our culture and community be? This was an urban societal problem in the first century that became a church problem. That rings a familiar bell for most of us. Who are you called to reach that you haven't? Refugees? Foster children? Children of addicts? Those living in poverty? For me, those are the faces that run through my mind. It may be different for you. If you're going to equate the Hellenistic widows to the culture today, consider the reasons that they were outcasts. They were from a different culture and spoke differently. They looked and acted different than the tradition of the community the disciples were ministering in. Many believe that the Hebrew Jews held more tightly to the laws of the Torah, whereas the Greek Jews were more liberal. Do you have people in your church who look, speak, and act differently? What about outside of your church? Do you have people who break from tradition, who are harder to find, who may not be inside the four walls of your church? Are you called to minister to them? You see Jesus address this with the disciples.

"Go therefore and make disciples of all the nations, baptizing them in the name of the Father and the Son and the Holy Spirit, teaching them to observe all that I commanded you" (Matthew 28:19a).

When Jesus sends you, He clearly sends you to disciple *all*, not some. Not the more convenient ones. Not the louder ones. Not the ones who sound or act the same. But *all*. I admit, that can be overwhelming. But if you're committed to letting go of the things you are not called to do, in exchange for clinging to what you are called to do, I believe you will see greater things in your ministry than you ever thought possible. As you strive to move from a susceptible ministry to a sustainable one, it is my prayer that you see the overlooked as not just a burden of the heart, but as part of the family in Christ.

"There is neither Jew nor Greek, there is neither slave nor free man, there is neither male nor female; for you are all one in Christ Jesus" (Galatians 3:28, NASB).

Things to Consider:

1. Is the ministry I am a part of, right now, susceptible or sustainable? Why?

2. Is there a disconnect between my intentions and my reality?

3. What do I need to let go of in order to grasp what I am called to hold onto?

4. Who might I be overlooking because I am overworked? How can I change that?

Rachael Groll is the Children's and Outreach Pastor at Living Waters Church in Meadville, PA. Her book, *GO,* was published last year, and has served as a resource and inspiration for those seeking to develop and implement their own outreach ministries.

chapter 16

BECOME A CHESS MASTER

Creating a staff team in kids' ministry

BY STEVEN KNIGHT

HAVE YOU EVER PLAYED CHECKERS? Checkers is a fun and simple game that people of all ages can enjoy together. The goal of checkers is to win by moving your pieces forward, capturing your opponents' checkers, and being the last one standing on the board. There's strategy involved, but it's not very complicated, especially when compared to a game like chess. Chess is an exciting game, but it takes time and energy to learn the rules, the strategies, and how to play it well. However, once you learn how to play chess, it can be very fun!

Creating a staff team in kids' ministry is more similar to playing chess than checkers. It's very strategic. You want to make the right moves at the right time.

In this chapter, we'll focus on creating a staff team of both paid and volunteer leaders. If you're in a small church, you're most likely talking about recruiting some key volunteers and empowering them for ministry. If you're in a medium-size church or larger, you can begin to open the conversation about hiring paid staff roles while also empowering key volunteers. We won't have time to cover how to build an entire volunteer team, but hopefully you'll get a better picture about how to create a kids' ministry staff team that includes both staff members and key volunteer leaders.

Ready to build your dream team?

CREATE YOUR TEAM STRATEGICALLY

The first step to creating a staff team in your kids' ministry is to determine the needs. What isn't getting done, or what is getting done that needs to be delegated to someone else? Start by writing out a list of these needs, including what might be needed in the next 1-2 years. What tasks do you have that need to be delegated to someone else? Are there areas in your kids' ministry that need a key leader?

If you're not sure how to create a list of those needs, start writing out all of the current kids' ministry responsibilities, including yours. Ask yourself: What are the tasks on this list that only I can do? Which tasks am I uniquely gifted to do? Your job description will have some necessary responsibilities that only you can do. However, there might be some tasks on this list that can be delegated.

As the ministry grows in size, you'll also move from being a "hands-on leader" to a "player-coach leader." A hands-on leader is very involved in everything that happens on a Sunday, Wednesday, and other key times of the week. A player-coach leader has some hands-on involvement, but they spend more time coaching the people who are directly involved in carrying out the ministry. For example, a player-coach leader would help coach kids' ministry teachers as they develop their teaching skills and use them regularly in the kids' ministry.

Once you have a list of responsibilities that you would like to delegate, you then have to consider if you need to hire a staff member or a key volunteer. Determine if the responsibilities can be completed by volunteers. If it makes sense to do that, then it's time to start recruiting!

Sometimes, you have some tasks that cannot be completed by a volunteer or a team of volunteers. If not, then ask yourself: Can a current staff member take on this responsibility and delegate something else?

I rarely meet a ministry leader who gets bored. After all, there's always something else to do in ministry! In some situations, though, it makes sense for another staff member to absorb some responsibilities. This can take place if they delegate more of their responsibilities or if their weekly hours are raised.

Occasionally, you will face a situation where you have a list of responsibilities that you cannot delegate to volunteers or transfer to another staff member. It just doesn't make sense to give someone more hours to take on those responsibilities. So, what should you do? The only remaining option may be to hire a new staff member.

SHOULD YOU HIRE A STAFF MEMBER?

Are you in that place? If you're seriously considering hiring a new staff member, here are a few questions to ask yourself.

How do other churches staff their ministries? Looking at slightly larger churches will help provide some ideas for how you could staff your team. At what point do other churches hire an administrative assistant? Do they have multiple kids' ministry directors for different age groups? As your church gets bigger, you'll want to look at increasingly specialized roles with a "team leader" to oversee them (Associate Pastor, Family Pastor, Kids' Director).

Is your church trying to do too much? Ask yourself this question as you evaluate your ministries and their effectiveness. Just because a ministry program is a good one doesn't mean you should keep doing it. Too much of a good thing can be bad for your church! If you can't afford to add new staff to help with the current responsibilities, then the answer might be to reduce the number of ministry programs or to simplify them in order to reduce the number of staff hours needed to run them.

Do you feel a call to start or develop a ministry area? If God is calling you to start a ministry or further develop a ministry area, then perhaps it's time to consider if a staff member is needed to make that happen.

How would this hire affect the volunteer team? Would hiring a staff member be seen as a positive move? Would this new staff member help equip the volunteer team for ministry?

Do you need a team leader or a specialist? Determine which one you need and that will determine how they will impact the rest of your staff team and volunteer team. You can't always avoid the need to hire a specialist, but that's typically an easier position to staff with a volunteer on your team, especially for small and medium-size churches. Team leaders could be volunteers, but often churches choose to spend more of their staffing budget first on team leaders, then hire the specialists that they don't have but need to sustain their ministries.

THE RIGHT PEOPLE ...

How do you find someone to fill your staff or key volunteer role? How do you begin to build a team that utilizes everyone's gifts for your team's greater purpose? When I interview candidates for a staff ministry position, here are a few key elements I consider.

The Six Cs:

- **Character:** Where are they in their spiritual growth? Are they faithful, available, and teachable?
- **Chemistry:** Would they work well with the staff team?

- **Competency:** What skills would they bring to the position and the team?
- **Culture:** Do they fit with the DNA of our church?
- **Calling:** Are they called to this ministry role?
- **Capacity:** Are they able to handle the schedule and responsibilities for this position?

No one will be perfect in all six areas. However, give each candidate you interview a rating between 1 and 5. If you have some 3s, 4s, and 5s, then there might be some potential with that candidate. If they rank lower in multiple categories, then they might not be the right person for the role, or at least, they're not a good fit for the role yet.

How do you determine how to rank candidates on this scale? It all comes down to asking questions. Interview them. Ask their references specific questions. If you can, talk to his or her spouse or other staff members who know them. Try to learn as much as you can about them.

Keep in mind that some categories are more important than others. For example, it's much easier to teach skills than it is to shape character.

If you want to create a volunteer leadership position that oversees a large area of ministry or a group of volunteers, then I still suggest you consider assessing their fit using the Six Cs. You probably won't interview them, but you should at least observe them in your ministry area, spend time getting to know them, and ask other staff and volunteers about them.

THE RIGHT PEOPLE ... IN THE RIGHT ROLES ...

Have you heard the phrase, "We need to make sure everyone is on the bus"? It means that you need to make sure your team is aligned and working towards the same mission, vision, and objectives. The best ministry teams have a unified team culture and work collaboratively.

Your team also needs to be in the right seats. Let me give you an example.

You're interviewing two candidates for a staff position. The first candidate is fantastic. She's an experienced, charismatic leader who seems to have excelled at everything she's done. She has spoken at large events, led large teams of volunteers, and written many books. She has great people skills.

The second candidate is pretty good, but he doesn't seem to have that perfect balance of charismatic stage presence, administrative skills, counseling aptitude, and organizational leadership that you're looking for. In fact, his top skills seem to be administrative skills.

Who do you hire? It depends on the position. For example, if you need a staff member whose responsibilities are mostly administrative, then candidate #2 is probably the right choice. It might hurt to give up the "perfect candidate" because candidate #1 seems so likeable, but candidate #2 would be a better fit for the role.

What about your existing teams? You could have some great people on your staff team, but they might be in the wrong roles. This can happen either with 1) a bad hire, or 2) a church that has grown in size, but the staff members have not grown themselves as their roles have grown.

It's better to be proactive and figure out how to get everyone in the right seat on the bus. The first step is to try to help staff members grow into their role. This works well if they have gifts and passions that they didn't know they had, simply because they never had the opportunity to use them.

The second step, if your staff members aren't growing into their roles, is to consider if they might be a good fit for a different staff position in the church. If so, that's great! If not, then you might need to make a tough decision to transition someone off the staff team.

THE RIGHT PEOPLE ... IN THE RIGHT ROLES ... AT THE RIGHT TIME

Hiring staff members or promoting key volunteers in a ministry at the right time is very important. Don't wait until your current staff is working double time in order to keep everything going. That means you're already way past the point of needing help!

Also, unless you feel God's call to start a new ministry, then there's no reason to hire anyone if you don't have any clear needs. Work with your senior leadership team to determine when is the right time to hire another staff member.

When you're looking for that new staff member or key volunteer, take the time you need to find the right person. Don't hire too fast before vetting the candidate. If you hire the wrong person, it will cost more and be more painful in the long run than if you had waited a few more months or longer to find the right candidate.

KIDS' MINISTRY ROLES

Here's a list of ideas for potential kids' ministry roles, either staff or volunteer. You likely don't need to hire or recruit for all of these roles, but prayerfully consider if any of them might be a good addition to your team. Your church's needs will vary based on the number of kids compared to the number of adults.

Small Church (0-200):

Kids' Director
Nursery Coordinator

Medium Church (200-400):

Same positions, plus ...
Early Childhood Director
Kids' AV Technician
Kids' Worship Leader
Kids' Large Group Teachers

Large Church (400-800):

Same positions, plus ...
Elementary Director
Kids' Welcome Coordinator
Kids' Ministry Administrative Assistant
Family Ministry Administrative Assistant
Kids' Team Leaders

Much Larger Churches (800+):

Same positions, plus ...
Intermediate Director
Kids' Large Group Coordinator
Kids' Worship Director
Kids' Large Group Teacher
Kids' Drama Leader
Age-Specific Director roles (ex: K-1st Grade Director)

... and more!

THE SEARCH PROCESS FOR A STAFF MEMBER

How do you find a new staff member for your team? Here are four methods for finding candidates for your open staff position.

First, start with your current team. Is there someone on the staff team who you can promote or give more responsibilities to? Or, do you have a volunteer who might be a good fit? If you have focused on leadership development in your ministry, then you might be able to hire from within.

A second method for finding candidates is to look in your church. Perhaps, someone serving in another ministry would be a great fit for this position. There might be a volunteer with amazing administrative abilities who is serving in the hospitality ministry. That person might be a good fit for your administrative assistant position! If you aren't familiar with everyone in your church, then bring a job description to your other staff members and ask if they know anyone in the church who might be a good fit. Advertise the position to your church and see who applies for it. Someone might be looking for a job, considering a career change, or wants to leave the corporate world, and your staff opportunity could be the perfect match.

If you can't find someone in your church who would be a good fit, start to look outside your church. Network with other churches and ask them if they know anyone who might be a good fit for the position. If you have a Bible college or seminary nearby, post the position on their job board. Look for ways to find out if someone in your community might be interested. If they already live in your community, then they will likely be more interested in living long-term in that area.

If you don't find any good candidates locally, then consider posting the position on church staffing job boards online or working with a church staffing company to find some good candidates. If your ministry needs a culture change, then hiring from the outside is likely the best option for your church. Remember, the most impressive resumes don't always equate to the best candidates. Use the Six Cs to determine who you should interview for your staff position.

READY TO PLAY CHESS?

Creating a staff team in kids' ministry takes time, prayer, planning, and intentionality. Are you ready? With a little hard work, you can build an incredible kids' ministry team that will make a significant impact in the lives of kids and families!

Steven Knight is a family pastor, a family ministry speaker, and the founder of KidminTools.com. He enjoys equipping ministry leaders almost as much as he enjoys a good cup of coffee.

chapter 17

TURN THE KEY

How to use personality assessments in leadership

BY ANGELA SANGALANG

"Knowing yourself unlocks your leadership potential. Conversely, a lack of self-awareness will hurt your leadership potential before it gets off the ground." (The Life Giving Leader, Tyler Reagin)

I AM AN INFP, 4w5 WHO SPEAKS IN GIFTS. Say what now? If you understand none of that, don't worry! I'll explain later. For now, just know they are the results of my top three favorite personality assessments.

I love taking personality assessments. I think they're fun and teach me a lot about myself. They help me become more self-aware, understand why I react a certain way to different situations, and even reveal my flaws and how I can become a healthier version of me. Getting to know how God created me gives me so many personal benefits, and for years, that's all they gave me.

Leaders know how to use the tools available to them to best lead people. Personality assessments are tools at your disposal. Taking them to grow personally is the first step. Turning the key is the second. Turning the key means using the results of your personality assessments to become a better leader.

As I've said, I am an INFP, 4w5 who speaks in Gifts. I am an INFP in the Myers-Briggs Type Indicator (MBTI), a Four Wing Five in the Enneagram, and my Love Language is Receiving Gifts. Since there are many personality assessments, I'm focusing on these three because I use them most often to turn the key. We'll start with the most commonly known personality assessment.

FIVE LOVE LANGUAGES

The Five Love Languages are five basic ways you perceive or feel love as outlined by Dr. Gary Chapman in his book *5 Love Languages*. The idea is that you have a primary love language, which can be: Words of Affirmation, Acts of Service, Receiving Gifts, Quality Time, and Physical Touch. Here's a quick explanation how a person feels loved by each love language.

- Words of Affirmation—Uses words to express love and appreciation

- Acts of Service—Does something to help you or take a load off your shoulders

- Receiving Gifts—Gives you meaningful and thoughtful gifts

- Quality Time—Spends quality time with you

- Physical Touch—Expresses love through physical touch like hugs

Problems arise when people don't understand their own and their loved one's love language. A husband whose love language is Words of Affirmation believes telling his wife how much he loves and appreciates her shows he loves her. However, if the wife's love language is Acts of Service, those words won't mean as much to her as when he washes the dishes.

HOW TO USE IT IN YOUR LEADERSHIP

My primary love language is Receiving Gifts. I feel loved when a loved one gives me a meaningful and thoughtful gift that tells me this person thought of me or knows my personality really well. It makes me feel known and that I matter. That's why I love to give gifts because I think it will make the recipient feel loved. That's why I agonize over volunteer gifts.

There's nothing wrong with volunteer gifts. The problem is, not every volunteer's love language is Receiving Gifts. My volunteers may not see gifts as a sign of love and appreciation. It's not enough to use volunteer gifts to show appreciation because Receiving Gifts is just one of five love languages. Use the different five love languages to express your thanks and love.

If your ministry team is small enough, you can survey them. Ask them to take the free Love Languages assessment (5lovelanguages.com), and use their love language to appreciate them. Here are some examples.

Love Language	Appreciation Ideas
Words of Affirmation	Send them a thank you card via snail mail
Acts of Service	Offer to run a non-ministry errand for them
Receiving Gifts	Give them their favorite candy bar
Quality Time	Take them out for coffee
Physical Touch	Give them high-5s and fist-bumps

If your ministry team is too big for one-on-one gestures, vary and alternate the ways you appreciate your volunteers as a team, using the different love languages. Turn the key! Speak the different love languages to better appreciate your ministry team and boost their morale.

MYERS-BRIGGS TYPE INDICATOR (MBTI)

The Myers-Briggs Type Indicator (MBTI) has roots in Carl Jung's theory of personality types and was developed by Katharine Cook Briggs and her daughter, Isabel Briggs Myers. It's a personality inventory that identifies 16 personality types that are a combination of these four pairs of psychological preferences: Extraversion (E) and Introversion (I); Sensing (S) and Intuition (N); Thinking (T) and Feeling (F); Judging (J) and Perceiving (P).

Preference Pairs	Deals With Your Preference To ...
Extraversion (E)	Focus on the outer world and social interaction
Introversion (I)	Focus on your inner world and solitary activities
Sensing (S)	Process information through the 5 senses
Intuition (N)	Process information through patterns and possibilities
Thinking (T).	Make decisions by considering objectivity, logic, and facts
Feeling (F)	Make decisions by considering personal concerns, harmony, and empathy
Judging (J)	Live a more structured and task-oriented lifestyle
Perceiving (P)	Live a more flexible and adaptable lifestyle

The 16 personality types are identified by an abbreviation of the letters representing one of the pairs in each of the Preference Pairs. I am an INFP. That means I prefer Introversion

(I), Intuition (N), Feeling (F), and Perceiving (P). You can find out your MBTI personality type by taking a free assessment online (16personalities.com). The MBTI helps you understand how you perceive the world and make decisions.

HOW TO USE IT IN YOUR LEADERSHIP

Understanding the different MBTI personality types will give you a better understanding of the people you lead and work with. However, there are 16 types and each type has its own strengths, weaknesses, values, work habits, and approach to relationships. Most people simply learn their own type and perhaps the types of spouses and children. Still, even only learning about my own type helps me as a leader. Here are some examples of what I learned as an INFP.

- Introversion (I): I prefer small groups and solitary activities, so I consciously make extra effort to meet parents, network with other ministry leaders, and hang out with my team.

- Intuition (N): I prefer to process information through possibilities which is great when dreaming big, but it means I temper my frustration if I meet challenges like budget and volunteer availability. I make the effort to be more pragmatic instead of only idealistic.

- Feeling (F): As a Feeling type, I prefer harmony and avoid confrontations, but that means putting on my big girl pants when problems arise with volunteers, families, or other church leaders. It means learning how to communicate objectively and with a thick skin.

- Perceiving (P): Oh the stories I could tell you about the times I frustrated my team with my preference for a flexible and adaptable lifestyle. It translates into winging it. It comes in handy if something unexpected spoils your plan, but it also means I'm sometimes the person throwing wrenches at the plan ... if I remember to make the plan. Creating structure and organization within my team and ministry is something I learned to do pretty quickly.

Once you understand your MBTI, use it to grow in your leadership by critically assessing your preferences and how they might affect those you lead and how you lead them. Each preference has a pair. Turn the key! Figure out how to lead with the other pair in consideration because chances are, you're leading people whose preferences are opposite yours.

ENNEAGRAM

The Enneagram is a personal discovery and growth tool that identifies nine basic personality types. The name comes from Greek where "ennea" means nine and "gram" means something written or drawn. The Enneagram is a circular diagram with nine points. Its origin is uncertain and disputed, which is why there is controversy about it within some Christian circles. The Enneagram we know today, however, has been developed and reframed over time as it spread and adapted into Western psychology.

The Enneagram's nine basic personality types are numbered, appropriately, one through nine. I am an Enneagram type Four or simply, a Four. You can find out your Enneagram number with a free assessment online at yourenneagramcoach.com, which translates the Enneagram through a Christian lens.

I am actually an Enneagram Four Wing Five (4w5). This means my main type is Four, but Enneagram types can be influenced or flavored by the types on either side of it. The numbers on either side of a Four are Three and Five. Like how the wings of a plane exist on either side of the body of the plane, a type Four has wings Three and Five on either side of it. When I say I am a Four Wing Five (4w5), I mean that I am a type Four who leans more towards my Five wing. The characteristics of a type Five adds flavor to my type Four characteristics.

Are you with me so far? It seems complicated and that's just the tip of the Enneagram iceberg, but that's one of the reasons I like the Enneagram. It doesn't simply categorize you into one type, but acknowledges that you go through seasons of life that affect the way you think, feel, and behave. However, more than just describing "how" you think, feel, and behave, the Enneagram describes the "why."

HOW TO USE IT IN YOUR LEADERSHIP

Having a language for the "why" behind the way I think, feel, and behave helps me grow as a person and as a leader. Here's an example. As a type Four, I love and value imagination and creativity because they speak into my desire (my "why") to be unique and special. In my capacity as a leader, I tend to look for other creative types because I respond to creativity. I've since learned to find people who are different from me— like my volunteer who's more focused on efficiency than creativity—and value their contributions to the team. My volunteer gets things done!

Here's another example. I don't like mundane and routine tasks because, as a type Four, I fear being ordinary and insignificant. As a leader, I tend to overlook the mundane and routine tasks like arranging furniture back to where it came from or wiping down the tables. My awesome team picks up where I slack without being told or asked. The Enneagram helps me recognize that these routine tasks may seem ordinary, but they're not insignificant. When my team pitches in to do the mundane, they're work is significant!

Use the Enneagram to learn not just "how" you think, feel, and behave, but also "why." It will help you recognize your biases and tendencies as a leader. It's like taking off rose-tinted glasses or the plank in your own eye. Only then can you see the value and worth of the people around you. You can see them how God sees them, and that's a great place to start leading them. Now you've turned the key!

There are many personality assessments out there. Take them and grow in your self-awareness. It's the first step towards unlocking your leadership potential, but take your results a step further. Use them as tools to understand how you lead and how you can become a better leader. Remember, turn the key!

Angela Sangalang is the Family Ministry Director in San Jose, CA, and writer of kidmintogether.com. She can be bribed with coffee, chocolate, and yarn. (She'll knit you a scarf if you ask nicely).

chapter 18

LOOKING FOR TIMOTHY
Engaging Kids in Leadership

BY CAROLYN NORKUS

"Let no one despise you for your youth, but set the believers an example in speech, in conduct, in love, in faith, in purity" (1 Timothy 4:12, ESV).

LACK OF VOLUNTEERS IS ALWAYS A HOT TOPIC at church ministry conferences and on ministry forums. Kids' ministry is probably at the top of the list of ministries that is always looking for more help. An often overlooked and very fertile soil to pick from is kids and students. Kids can take your ministry from good to great, from a slow burn to on fire, from head knowledge to living out God's Word.

Let's start with students: middle and high school kids. Students bring a certain level of energy and coolness to a ministry that adults just can't do. They are closer in age to what kids are looking forward to becoming. To a kid, they represent the "when I get bigger." Allowing students to take key roles in your ministry models to kids what it means to live out their faith and to practice what they are learning.

People want to feel significant and kids are no different. They want to be seen, heard, valued, and respected. Too often the job in kids' ministry is perceived as one where you download on them as much biblical information as you possibly can and get them to a place where they say the prayer of accepting Jesus. I believe your job is so much more. It's more than just biblical knowledge. It's what they do with that knowledge. It's more than them reciting a prayer, but it's the beginning of a relationship. One of the most successful ways I've found that helps kids mature and move through the discipleship journey is by coaching—helping and leading them towards leadership.

Kids are blessed with spiritual gifts, just like adults. They have the same Holy Spirit living inside of them that lives inside you. When you begin to look at kids as brothers and sisters in Christ, you can see they have the same potential to make a spiritual impact on their peers as the adult leaders do.

Remember kindergarten? Kindergarten had a list of roles that kids couldn't wait to fill: line leader, taking things to the office, watering the plants, counting the hot lunches needed, taking attendance. Kids love to help! So why don't you let them help? Why do you shy away from allowing them to lead? You have to be honest with yourself here, because it's probably that you don't want to let go of the control. It won't get done like you thought it would or should, but does that really matter?

Studies show that people who visit a church are more likely to stay if they get connected by serving and/or are part of a group. Why would kids be any different? Kids will come to church because their parents make them, but sometimes families come because the kids can't stand the thought of missing church. As a parent, I know it's a lot easier going somewhere when my kids want to go and not because I'm making them go. If you, a kids' ministry leader, created opportunities for kids to belong to a group and they had an opportunity to serve or lead, you could help families "stick" to your church. Here are some steps to lead kids towards leadership.

SET THEM UP TO BE SUCCESSFUL

When you have decided that you're going to give kids leadership roles, you want to set them up for success. Give them clear expectations. You can't expect kids to instinctually do things that an adult would, because they aren't adults. They haven't had the life experiences to give them those instincts. Be clear with them and explain what exactly it is you want them to do. Make no assumptions. Give them as much information as you can and often.

Utilizing the "I do, we do, you do" approach works well here. "I do." The first time you have them do something, they should only observe. Give them something to fill out or have them write down what they observed to keep their attention. "We do." The next time, do the job together, giving them pointers along the way, correcting, and encouraging. "You do." Finally, you observe them. This time give as much encouragement as possible and save any correction for a debrief at the end. Depending on the job you have asked them to do, some of these steps may take a couple of practices before moving on to the next.

Trust them enough to allow them to make mistakes. Everyone makes mistakes. It's usually when you learn the most. So trust them to try their best, but know that they may stumble. This is also an amazing time when they get to witness your trust and learn about grace and forgiveness. Before you address the concern, check yourself to make sure you're going to talk to them with a teaching spirit. You can show them Jesus in this moment. Share with them where they mis-stepped, how they can correct it if needed, and encouragement to do better next time. Leaders grow when they are allowed to try and when they learn from their mistakes.

HELP THEM FIND THE RIGHT FIT

Kids can have spiritual gifts too. Help them discover their gifts and use them. Just like adults, some will love to shine in the spotlight while others will prefer to help behind the scenes. Some will love to work with other kids, some will feel comfortable around adults, while others will prefer not to work with many people. Talk with them and get to know their passions and what they spend their time doing. Talk with their parents or guardians to see what gifts they feel their child has. Let them know that you see some great potential in them. Share with them that you want to help them find a way to use their skills and gifts to serve the kingdom. I guarantee that will be a fun conversation to have. Not only will you be shepherding a kid in your ministry, but you will be finding ways to benefit the ministry and the kingdom all while connecting with and encouraging a parent. Win, win, win!

Give kids age appropriate roles. Take some time to pull a few other adult leaders together to brainstorm ways kids can lead and serve. What are some of the tasks that could be given to the kids of your church? Make a list and attach an age range that would appropriately fit. Get creative here. There's probably a plethora of tasks that you or your team does. Could it be something that you give a kid to do? For example, every Sunday morning we play music on an iPad with a Bluetooth speaker in our kids' ministry hallway. One day, someone asked one of our fifth grade boys if he would mind running to my office and grabbing the iPad and speaker I had forgotten on my desk. He was elated to help and to be trusted with the equipment. Honestly, I wasn't looking for a way to help this boy into leadership, but I am thankful for the leader who asked and the Holy Spirit who prompted. We showed him how to turn it all on and sign into our Spotify account. He was then asked if he would like this job. He eagerly agreed to take on the responsibility. I was told later by his mother that her son was so excited to be asked to help and he told her that they had to be sure to be early to church because he had a job to do.

OFFER OPPORTUNITIES FOR THEM TO IMPROVE

There are several areas that you can cover to help kids improve on their leadership skills. Creating fun and engaging times to work on skills not only will improve them, but will also build relationships and help unite your kids' ministry team.

Communication. Not many kids are natural communicators. Kids can benefit from being coached on ways to communicate. They are growing up in a generation where face-to-face communication isn't always common. They communicate more through pictures and texts than they do through conversations. Creating times for them to practice "small talk" or greeting people as they enter a room will help them become more comfortable and confident. Get them comfortable with making eye contact. Again, this doesn't come naturally. Many adults struggle with making eye contact. Demonstrate for them what it's like to talk with someone who makes eye contact and someone who doesn't.

Confidence. Self-confidence comes from a sense of competence. A confident kid will have a positive and realistic perception of his or her abilities. Offering words of encouragement can help develop this confidence, especially when you refer to the kid's specific efforts or abilities. Let them know that they are bound to make mistakes and that's okay. Assure them that you will be there to coach and help them improve when that happens.

Integrity. Teach them and help them understand that what they do and say, even when they think no one is looking, says a lot about their character and their integrity. When they have been given a leadership role, they must understand that it's a privilege. It's a high calling and their actions are not only accountable to you but to God. They are representing Christ when they serve in a leadership role.

Accountability. When you hold a kid accountable for the job they've been given, it's not being mean. It's actually showing them you care. When you call them out for slacking on their responsibilities, you're telling them that what they do matters ... that they matter. They let the team or ministry down when they don't follow through or do a poor job. All of this shows a kid that they can make a difference, good or bad. Again this must be done with a teaching spirit through love and grace, but do it. Hold them accountable. They deserve to know that they're important enough to be noticed when they haven't done what was entrusted to them.

CELEBRATE THEM

Celebrate them as a whole group of kid leaders and celebrate them individually. Celebrate them amongst their peers as well as in front of older generations. There are lots of ways you can celebrate kids. Food is always a winner, but kids will appreciate a handwritten note in the mail just as much. Make a video of all your kid leaders serving and share it with your church family during a service. Showcase them on social media (with parents' permission). Write a note to their parents about the growth or skills you see in their child and share with them how they bless the kids' ministry. Be creative. It doesn't have to cost a lot of money, but do something and do it often.

This is a great cross-generational opportunity, too. Enlist the senior members of your church family to be spiritual buddies with your kid leaders. Have them write notes of encouragement to your kid leaders. Make a space for them to meet and pray together before they serve on a Sunday morning. It's another way you can show a kid that they matter to the whole church.

GROW THEM

"Our ceiling should be the next generation's floor." – (Brian Houston, Senior Pastor and Global Founder of Hillsong Church) I love this statement because it charges us, the current leaders, to grow leaders. You serve a big, big God. How could you possibly imagine that you have taken the ministry in which you serve as far or as big as God wants it to be? Our job does not stop when you've helped someone find a place to serve. Everyone has a next step in their discipleship journey. You must continue to find ways and opportunities for kids to take next steps. Maybe that begins with helping them develop spiritual disciplines, showing them how to share their faith, or discovering and building on their spiritual gifts. Not every church's discipleship process will look the same, but have a plan and walk them through it.

Every child is made in the image of God. If you saw the potential in kids that God sees in them, you would see kids with the ability to lead and to serve the Kingdom. God has a calling on their life, just as He has a calling on yours. What an honor and a privilege it is to be used by God to help kids connect with Him and step into their calling.

"And let us not grow weary of doing good, for in due season we will reap, if we do not give up" (Galatians 6:9, ESV).

Carolyn Norkus is the Kids' Ministry Director at Chapel Pointe Church in Hudsonville, MI. The best thing you can do is introduce kids to Jesus and Carolyn is blessed to have that be her job for the last 8 years. She loves to laugh and kid jokes are her favorite.

chapter 19

SNAPCHAT, INSTAGRAM, TWITTER—OH MY!

Developing teen leaders

BY SANDY HALL

IN A WORLD THAT OFTEN MEASURES one's worth by how many likes their photo or comment receives, kids' ministry leaders need to remind the kids you serve and the teens who serve alongside you, that their worth is measured by God's love for them and not by how many clicks they're able to generate.

Teens today are bombarded with social media images and comments that can make them feel like less than they are, and that promote the belief they have to be someone else in order to be liked or loved. They are also part of a generation being raised with values that can easily foster feelings of entitlement—that they can do whatever they want. It's all about them, not others. They need a place not only to come to, but to serve and to learn that they are worth so much more than the world says they are. They need a place to become leaders and champions of our Lord and Savior. They need a church home where they humble themselves before God and serve others, a place where it's not always about them.

You may ask, "Don't we already have enough to do just developing the kids in our ministry? Now we also need to take on the growth and development of the teens who serve?" The resounding answer to this question is, "YES!" You need to pour into these teens as if they were your own children. During my years in kids' ministry, I saw so many broken, hurting teens who came to know Christ through serving in kids' ministry. These teens developed relationships with other Christian adults they served alongside and those adults helped them navigate this secular world with love and encouragement.

If you walk into any Sunday kids' ministry class, I can guarantee you that if there is a teen leader present, the kids are surrounding him or her. Teens tend to have a special connection to the kids that's not always possible with even the best adult leaders. These teens are the ones the kids want to talk to, be near, and be totally honest with. The kids think these teens are "cool." Chances are that the teachers don't ever get the title of "cool"!

So, how do you go about developing teen leaders? Below is a simple 5-step process to accomplish just that.

Work with your Student Ministry Pastor/Director. *"Two are better than one; because they have a good reward for their labor"* (Ecclesiastes 4:9, NASB). Establish a good working relationship with your student pastor/directors as they are the ones with a wealth of teens at their disposal. They know these teens and can partner with you in asking them to serve. At the same time an opportunity is provided to be of help when things arise in these teens' lives where they could use help or assistance.

Have a teen representative on your kids' ministry executive board. *"Let no one look down on your youthfulness, but*

SNAPCHAT, INSTAGRAM, TWITTER—OH MY!

rather in speech, conduct, love, faith and purity, show yourself an example of those who believe" (1 Timothy 4:12, NASB). This is monumentally important. Teens need to have a voice in your leadership. They need to know that you value their ideas and opinions, and that they matter to your kids' ministry future planning. You can do this in two ways:

- Approach a teen who you have seen growing and thriving in your ministry and ask them to be on the board.

- Have teens apply for that position through an application and interview process.

This is a great way to get to know the teens and understand what is truly in their hearts. You also need to invest your time and energy into developing your teen leaders because the future of your ministry depends on cultivating new volunteers every season. These kids can help you spread the word when it comes time to recruit, and no one understands social media better than the teens of today. In addition, teens are more likely to volunteer if asked by a peer to join them. They will be your best sales people for your ministry, if they feel valued and loved.

Get to know the teens in your ministry. *"Therefore, confess your sins to one another, and pray for one another so that you may be healed. The effective prayer of a righteous man can accomplish much"* (James 5:12, NASB). This may seem like a no-brainer, but it can easily get away from you. Invite them to visit you in your office, ask them out for coffee, invite them to kids' ball games or recitals. You'll be surprised how many teens will show up if they are just invited! There is nothing more awesome than seeing the faces of those kids when their teen leader shows up at one of their events!

You may dislike social media, but the reality today is social media is sometimes the only way to engage with some of your teens. Create for yourself a Snapchat, Instagram, and Twitter account. Educate yourself on social media etiquette and follow the teens who serve in your ministry. Never embarrass them online. If they post something inappropriate, schedule a time to meet with them in person to discuss. You'll come to find that many times when something inappropriate has been posted, it's because they were hurting. What a great time to pour into them and see where their heart is and what the Bible teaches about your bodies and your words. Obviously, social media is the easiest because you can see what they are up to and send them encouragement at the drop of a hat. Unfortunately, you can also see when they're making big mistakes (posting inappropriate pictures or comments). Your first instinct is to correct them on their post, which only serves to have them embarrassed, humiliated, or they will just block you from seeing anything in the future. You need to remind these teens that you're not here to judge them, but you will in a loving, Christlike way always point them back to God and what His Word says. Sometimes, you may be all they have.

Train, Train, Train. *"Where there is no guidance the people fall, but in abundance of counselors there is victory"* (Proverbs 11:14, NASB). Make sure you include teens in any and all of your training for kids' ministry. Share with them your vision for the ministry. They are an integral part of your team and they need to be trained just as your adult leaders need to be trained. If budget allows, invite them along to a kids' ministry conference or put on a mini-conference for them at your church. It doesn't have to be anything fancy, maybe a one-day training where they are taught teaching methods and strategies to help the kids in your ministry. Do not look at them as "gophers" for your ministry. Invest the time in training them beyond the gopher-position, because they are more likely to be the future adult volunteers of your ministry if they feel appreciated and trained now.

Engage adult kids' ministry leaders on your team to assist you with your teens. *"Go therefore and make disciples of all the nations, baptizing them in the name of the Father and* *the Son and the Holy Spirit"* (Matthew 28:19, NASB). It may seem overwhelming to add more training, developing, and leading to your to-do list, but the great news is you don't have to do it alone! You have adult leaders within your ministry who you can tap to help or even oversee the teen component of your kids' ministry.

The statistics of teens leaving the faith when they finish high school is alarming. According to the Public Religion Research Institute, of kids/teens raised in a religion, 62% say they abandoned their childhood faith before they turned 18, and 28% between the ages of 18-29. According to an article written by Kelsey Dallas, "Why Teens Leave the Faith and What Churches and Families are Doing About It," "Youth programs are most successful at drawing teenagers to religious belief when they help them see 'faith in action.'" What better faith in action than serving others. By the teens serving in your kids' ministry, they will not only be a part of something bigger than themselves, but they're more likely to remain in church after they've left for college!

You need to also realize that these teens may come to church by themselves. They were invited by a friend and have continued coming despite their parents not attending. If they are coming alone, they may have no Christian guidance at home. These teens need you and your ministry even more? These are the teens who are hungry to serve, to have a Christian family, to have adults they can talk to and who will be honest, loving, and encouraging towards them. What an opportunity to show these teens Christ's love.

In my years in ministry, I have mentored several teens and I've had the privilege of seeing my adult volunteers mentor the teens they serve with. They need us; they may not be receiving Christ-like love at home and it's our job to show it to them. They become like our own children. You miss them when they leave for college. You continue to pray for them. You try to stay in contact with them when they go away. This is another important aspect of developing your teen leaders. Keeping in contact in some form or fashion with them when they leave. Whether it's through phone calls, letter writing, or social media, you need to continue to be in their lives. This is the time to reach out, whether they went to college down the road or 2,000 miles away. A phone call from a trusted Christian mentor will go a long way to help the teens get back on track.

"A good man leaves an inheritance to his children's children ..." (Proverbs 13:22, NASB). An inheritance in not only about money; it can also be an inheritance of values, character, and wisdom for the glory of God. You need to see your teen leaders as the future of your ministry. You never know, one of them may be the next kids' ministry pastor/director. Train them well to be able to lead the future. *"Train up a child in the way he should go, Even when he is old he will not depart from it"* (Proverbs 22:6, NASB).

Sandy Hall has a Masters in Marriage and Family Therapy. She is an editor for Lifeway Kids' curriculum, "Bibles Studies for Life." Sandy is the former Kids' Ministry Director at West Pines Community Church. She's wife to Ed and mama to two adult children, Amanda and Dylan. If you want to make her happy, give her anything that's pink and sparkly!

chapter 20

SHAKE IT OFF
Lessons from AirBnB, Scott Frost, and Taylor Swift

BY AANNA SMALLEY

I'VE STARTED USING AIRBNB a lot more often when vacationing. On our most recent trip, my husband and I rented a poolside cabana in sunny San Diego. This was by far my most favorite vacation rental experience. We had access to an outdoor kitchen, bonfire, huge in-ground pool (which included a giant flamingo floaty named "Pinky"), and outdoor dining area. To top it off, the house sat up on a bluff that overlooked much of San Diego and even all the way south to Tijuana. It was picture perfect.

I'd read reviews before booking this place and all were positive! One former renter said she reserved the place for an entire month and used it as an "author's hide-away" while she worked on her book. It took me minutes of being there to decide I wanted to stay long term.

Sometimes, it really is just that easy! You see something you love, research a little more about it, and determine in a heartbeat that This. Is. For. You.

But it's not uncommon for that excitement, determination, and newness to wear off as you encounter the uglier side of a job. Church work is not for the faint of heart. It can leave you battered and bruised, tired and defeated, worn out and feeling worthless. No one wants to be in that position. So how can you maintain that shiny, new feeling you had when initially stepping into your ministry job? How do you find enjoyment in the everyday tasks? What makes you want to stick it out long term?

I've been working at my church for nearly 10 years now. I came in a doe-eyed college senior for an internship that was set to last for five months. A position opened up in the kid-min department and I chased it down. I loved working here! I'd been able to flex my creative muscle repeatedly. I'd been given the opportunity to begin new programs, reinvent others, teach large group, connect with parents/kids/volunteers, try new things and fail in a safe environment. It was fast-paced and new. The church had grown, was continuing to grow, and it was so fun! I couldn't imagine a day when I'd come in and not love every single thing about my job.

Toward the end of my first year I got called into my boss's boss's office. Yeah. That's never a good thing. As I sat with him and with my boss he described to me an email that had been sent to the senior pastor in regards to communication I'd had with a volunteer. I can, to this day, tell you exactly what my email said and exactly why I was told it didn't come across well.

I was crushed.

That was the first day that I didn't want to be at work.

And yet, 10 years later I'm still here. I keep showing up. Why? Because I've figured out that staying long term is worth it.

Ed Young said, "Ministry is brutiful." I really believe there's not a truer statement. It has moments of beauty (kids accepting Jesus, babies being dedicated by families committed to raising them in Christ, parents growing more and more confident in their ability to lead their families well spiritually) and moments when it's brutal (dealing with sickness and death, having tough conversations with volunteers or those you serve, and of course receiving criticism). You have to dig for those moments of beauty! That's why I think one of the very best things that's kept me serving at the same church for nearly 10 years is remembering what I love.

I find that one of the easiest way to keep these loves at the forefront of my mind is to list them out. I'd encourage you to do this, too. Write out a list of the 10 things you love most about your job. This may be something that comes really easily for you. I also understand that you might be in a place where you're struggling to come up with one thing you love about your job. So start with the very basics. Do you like your work schedule? Do you like having time off? Do you like giving kids high-5s on a Sunday morning? Write that down! Don't stop until you get a list of 10 things written out. It's okay to think on it for a few days.

I also want to encourage you in this: if you truly can't identify 10 things you love about your job, think back to the things you used to love about your job and write those out. Make your focus pointed toward getting back to a place where you get to do some of those things again.

As my role has morphed, grown, and changed along with our church, I've had to let go of some things I really loved doing. I've also made certain to always try to maintain a handful of the things that bring me the most joy! My boss, our senior pastor, has been wise in also encouraging me to do this. My most recent role change moved me from being the KidMin Pastor who oversaw the kidmin pastors for each of our campuses as well as all elementary programming to the NextGen Pastor where I now oversee the Lead KidMin and Lead Student Ministry Pastors. Many of the creative elements I loved about my job are no longer part of what I do. But as I made this transition, my senior pastor and I sat down and talked through reasons why I'd be good at this new role. We also talked about things that are important to me. We both determined that if I lost all opportunities to communicate as a teacher, I'd eventually start to fall out of love with my job. So, we've found creative ways to make sure that I still have the opportunity to communicate whether it's writing curriculum, preaching during our student ministry service, or teaching at parenting conferences. I still love my job, 10 years in, because I've made sure to hang on to some of my first loves.

It's okay to have those conversations with your leadership. If you find that your role has morphed and changed, or you've handed over many of your responsibilities and you're finding that you have let go of all of the things you loved most, it's okay to explore the idea of taking some of those back!

There's no doubt there will be seasons where it feels like nothing is "good" in ministry. I've been there and I just encourage you to find your fire again! Remember what it is that you love and journey back to those things again.

I'm a Nebraska Cornhusker fan. This year has been a homecoming for our new head coach Scott Frost. We all remember the glory days when he played on a national championship team here and the entire state has been electric since he was hired back. But our season is now 0-4 for the first time since World War II. This is a "rebuilding year." Each game brings hope that we just might pull a win out and each game has ended with another loss. And yet, every Saturday the entire state dons scarlet and cream and 90,000+ people enter Memorial Stadium from all over the country. Why? Because we get that we're playing for the long game! We're not looking for an instant win under our new coach (though none of us would be mad if that happened). We're trusting and believing that Coach has what it takes to get these boys to a place where they are disciplined, consistent, and skilled, and we know that it takes time.

Ministry is no different. If you walked into a ministry expecting to turn it on its side, revamp, revitalize, and revolutionize what has happened at that church for decades and walk away at the end of the year getting high-5s and "atta boy" or "atta girl" statements thrown at you, you're going to be disappointed (and probably are also walking into that position for all the wrong reasons).

Ministry is a long game! It takes time to build up trust with the families you serve and with the volunteers who serve alongside you. Sure, you'll have some of those "early adaptors" who jump on your train the minute it arrives at the station, but for the most part, it takes time. I'd encourage anyone to develop a plan. Make a short term plan—things you can easily change or things that need changed immediately. Make a mid-range plan—where do you want to be next? And create a long term plan—what's your end goal here? Slowly and methodically invest. And when you get to the end of that long term plan, start over again. Make a new plan. Be energized by the completion of your very first set of goals, then go back to the drawing board and improve on what you've done! Challenge even the "good things" to see if they're good enough.

When people see that you will, in fact, do what you say you're going to do, they'll become more and more supportive. Their belief in you will grow. As they learn that your ideas are good, that they work, and that you have their very best interest in mind, you'll feel your cheering section grow, too.

I think it can be easy to come into a position and identify all of the things you'd like to change, but take notes from Coach Frost. Make decisions based on the long term goal, not based on your ability to make quick change. Don't be discouraged by the short game. Move intentionally and build up trust with your leadership, those who serve alongside you, and the parents and kids you serve. You know what? You're allowed to make mistakes. If you swing, miss, and fail to get it right the first time, you get to try again! Long game. Remember?

I think Taylor Swift holds the last key to staying long term. "Players gonna play ... haters gonna hate ... heartbreakers gonna break ... fakers gonna fake ..." This is so true in ministry as well. I grew up in a ministry family. My dad has been a pastor my entire life and continues to serve. (By the way, he's served the same church for 25 years.) My mom was a worship pastor for most of my middle school and high school years. My grandpa was a pastor. What I'm telling you is I've seen a lot of different people and situations in my experience with ministry. And Taylor's statements hold true. There will always be someone or something that seems to get in your way.

I could fill the rest of the book with stories of things I've experienced or my family has experienced in ministry that could easily have made any of us just pack it up and walk away. I've lost friends. I've watched people who work under me quit because of a problem they've had with me. I've been treated badly. I've been lied about. I've had people make entire Facebook pages just to drag me through the mud. My dad has experienced worse in ministry, and I'd be shocked if my grandpa didn't as well.

Yikes! I know this sounds like it's headed down a dark, twisty road, but I promise I'm not, because our why is so much bigger than these few nasty things that happen! Please don't throw in the towel when your feelings get hurt. I'm no dummy. Words cut like a knife, but you've got to learn to "shake it off, shake it off!"

I was in the midst of a really difficult circumstance in ministry a few years ago. My heart was broken by the situation. I was hurt by the way people were treating me, the staff at my church, and my friends who were involved. It was the darkest moment to date I've had in ministry. But God saw me there. He saw my hurt and He sat in it with me. When I was at the very bottom of all of it, He strategically reminded me that He called me to this job. I was reminded of my calling when Melissa delivered flowers to me with a card from her kids telling me they loved me. I was reassured again when Kim showed up with balloons and a kind note. Or when Kelly sat with me and told me she was praying me through this. And if you'd told me to "shake it off" in the midst of all of that, I would've scoffed. But in hindsight, that's exactly what I did.

Each day, I showed up, whether I felt like it or not. Each day, I was intentional in choosing one thing I loved about serving others as a career. Each day, I asked others to pray for me and I spent time with God, too. Slowly but surely, God placed the right people in my life to remind me of why I do what I do. There will always be nasty people. There will always be someone smarter than me. There will always be someone whose ideas outweigh mine or whose voice is louder, but there will also always be kids who meet Jesus for the first time, families making their faith matter, volunteers who finally see how their service is affecting kids and families, and so much more!

Staying long term anywhere in ministry takes guts. If you're reading this right now and thinking, "I'm not very brave. I don't really have any guts." I see you. I've been there too. I've wondered what business I had serving in ministry. Just as quickly as I've had those thoughts and feelings, I've reminded myself that Satan is a fantastic liar and he'll do whatever it takes to stop me from doing what God has called me to do.

If you're new to the church you're serving and can't imagine being in a place where you'd feel like you needed out, commit to memory the things you love most about ministry. Remind yourself of the hope you have in the next generation, and continue asking God to help you find joy in the serving.

"When you go through deep waters,

I will be with you.

When you go through rivers of difficulty,

> you will not drown.
> When you walk through the fire of oppression,
>> you will not be burned up;
>> the flames will not consume you.
> For I am the LORD your God,
>> the Holy One of Israel, your Savior"

(Isaiah 43:2-3a, NLT).

Commit to memory the things you love most about being in children's ministry. Revisit those often and remind yourself of the joy that comes from serving in this special area of the kingdom. Commit to stay for the long haul.

Aanna Smalley has been serving at StoneBridge Christian Church in Omaha, NE for nearly 10 years in a variety of different KidMin/NextGen roles! She loves her little family (husband Spencer and dog Millie), traveling, Husker football, Jazzercise, and a great cup of black coffee!

CPSIA information can be obtained
at www.ICGtesting.com
Printed in the USA
FFHW020538241118
49564011-53949FF